DMU
COMPENDIUM
COLIN BOOCOCK

The longest DMUs in the British Isles are the seven-car 'Meridian' units of Class 222 operated by East Midlands Trains. Originally built as nine-car sets, two intermediate vehicles from each set were removed to strengthen EMT's four-car Meridians to five cars. Seen here, No 222 003 approaches the outskirts of Derby on 4 July 2011, working the 09.27 from Sheffield to London St Pancras. Author

Ian Allan
PUBLISHING

Front cover photo: *These Class 150 units and their derivatives are among the DMU workhorses that have flooded the British rail scene in recent decades. In this 1990s view, Class 150/2 unit No 150 257 is about to cross the Tay Bridge running north towards Dundee.* Author

Back cover photos: *(Top) Two CIÉ AEC railcar sets head south through Killiney en route from Dublin to Bray in May 1959.* J. G. Dewing/Colour-Rail *(Bottom) This power car is part of the 'Bristol Pullman' service, caught by the camera at Bath Spa in June 1967.* Colour-Rail

A Northern Ireland Railways three-car DEMU calls briefly at Dhu Varren halt just south of Portrush on its way to the junction at Coleraine in May 1988. These diesel-electric units were a development of the BR Southern Region 'Hampshire' sets using BR mark 2-style carriages. Author

First published 2011

ISBN 978 0 7110 3506 5

Published by Ian Allan Publishing
an imprint of Ian Allan Publishing Ltd, Hersham, Surrey KT12 4RG.
Printed in England by Ian Allan Printing Ltd, Hersham, Surrey KT12 4RG.

Visit the Ian Allan Publishing website at www.ianallanpublishing.com

Distributed in the United States of America and Canada by BookMasters Distribution Services.

CONTENTS

Preface

This third book in the Compendium series covers diesel railcars and multiple-units in the British Isles. Because space permits it, the author has attempted to describe and detail every type of self-propelled passenger-carrying diesel rail vehicle on British and Irish national railways from the first in 1928 to the end of 2010.

The book uses three main descriptions for such vehicles: diesel railcar; diesel multiple-unit; railbus. The term 'railcar' is used to cover early vehicles that were often single cars, or had been derived from such vehicles or were otherwise unable to work in multiple. Also in Ireland the term 'railcar' is used where in the UK people would use the term 'diesel multiple-unit' and that difference of language use is reflected, at least in part, in this book. Otherwise, a 'diesel multiple-unit', shortened to 'DMU', is the terminology preferred by the author. There were many four-wheeled railcars and most of these are grouped under the term 'railbus'. Again there are exceptions to this, the main one being the inclusion of the BR 'Pacer' series units in the term 'DMU'; they were intended to be cheap DMUs and this is what they are generally called.

There have been several essays by railways and manufacturers into the DMU field over the years. Those vehicles that have subsequently led useful lives are included in the appropriate chapters. Those that ran only for short trial periods, or for only a year or two in traffic, are grouped in Appendix 1: Prototypes.

Many DMUs when withdrawn from traffic were subsequently transferred to departmental stock to undertake various tasks for railway engineers or operators. Appendix 2 – Departmental DMUs – details those that were either specially built for departmental work or were transferred there from operating stock, the former being detailed as much as possible, the latter just covered in summary, their details having already been printed in the appropriate chapters covering their earlier years.

Acknowledgements

It has been an interesting task to track down details and photographs of every type of DMU and diesel railcar or railbus in the British Isles. Without help from a wide group of photographers and experts this book would not be as definitive as it is. In the hope that I have not missed out anyone who made a supreme effort to help me, whether or not I have been able to use their material, I list and thank the following: Allan Baker, David Cable, Paul Chancellor of Colour-Rail, Ian Copplestone, David Coxon, Ian Dobson, Dick Fearn and Peter Smyth of Iarnród Éireann, Colm Flanagan, Charles Friel, Brian Morrison, David Percival, Peter Stanton, Peter Swift, Neil Tee of the Donegal Railway Heritage Centre, Michael Walsh, the Institution of Mechanical Engineers library staff, the Irish Railway Record Society (IRRS) and the National Railway Museum library staff at York. To all these I am extremely grateful. And where would we be without the excellent photographic resource of the Ian Allan library?

An Iarnród Éireann four-car Class 29000 awaits departure from Dublin Connolly with a service for the Maynooth line. These diesel-hydraulic units were built by CAF in Spain and are the main sustainers of commuter services in the Irish north-south corridor. Author

Most passenger trains in the British Isles in the 21st century are formed of multiple-units, or at least are unit train formations. This Compendium looks at the whole range of diesel multiple-units (DMUs) including their ancestors, the early diesel railcars. In addition to describing all British DMUs, this volume describes the Irish ones as well, because much of the early development and operational success of diesel railcars and multiple-units took place in Ireland. This book therefore acts as a companion to the author's earlier book, Locomotive Compendium: Ireland, as well as complementing the other books in this series. However, to make best use of the pages, this book does not cover railcars driven by steam or petrol even though many of these pioneered the railcar principle.

Prototypes

Experimental prototypes were many during the 20th century. Most did not make it into long-term regular service, and so are relegated to a section near the back of this book. This includes the very first diesel passenger unit train in the British Isles which the London Midland & Scottish Railway (LMS) experimented with in 1928. Several of these interesting vehicles might well have had a more positive future had the wars not intervened or had different people been in power on the railways at various times.

Beginnings

The oldest railcar in Ireland sits quietly at one side of the display hall in the Ulster Folk and Transport Museum at Cultra, east of Belfast on the Bangor line. The three-feet gauge County Donegal Railways (CDR) petrol railcar No 1 dates from 1906. Another exhibit in the same museum is diesel railcar No 10. This was sold by the Clogher Valley Railway to the CDR in 1941, a second-hand vehicle even then! No 10 embodied the style and engineering philosophy of the Wigan-based manufacturer Walker Brothers. The passenger saloon was like a bus

Early diesel railcar experiments occupied many railway engineers in the 1930s as railways probed the technical possibilities and economics of these vehicles. The firm of Armstrong Whitworth produced 3 single railcars, all of which had enough power to haul a trailer. This is the Lady Hamilton, *working in the northeast. Ian Allan library*

body with a rear bogie, the front of the saloon being articulated off the back of a long power bogie on which were mounted the engine and mechanical transmission and the driving cab. Being unidirectional, this type of railcar needed to be turned at the end of each trip – no hardship on a railway that still had turntables for its steam locomotive fleet. Such railcars continued to be supplied to Ireland until 1952 and provided the basic service on several secondary routes.

Other lines of diesel railcar development in the United Kingdom paralleled the Irish vehicles. Early UK diesel railcars mostly were not used for a significant length of time as the basic vehicles of any train service, at least not until the Great Western Railway began to populate its lines with its well-known diesel railcar fleet in the 1930s and 1940s. While the early GWR railcars used non-standard lightweight structures to enhance the vehicles' power-to-weight ratios, later ones were much more like standard carriages but fitted with diesel engines and transmissions underneath. The last four GWR railcars were built as single-ended vehicles and were matched with modified standard carriages to form, in effect, three-car multiple-units. Thus appeared the predecessors of what became much later a large fleet of DMUs on both sides of the Irish Sea. The progressive development of these cars is detailed in the appropriate section of this book.

First-generation DMUs

Once again, the story moves back to Ireland, this time on the 5ft 3in gauge system. In 1949 the Great Northern Railway (Ireland) purchased a fleet of diesel railcars from the Park Royal factory. These handsome main line railcars were formed into three-car and four-car sets using converted conventional carriages as trailers. Like the GWR cars, they had bus-type diesel engines, two per railcar, mounted on outriggers under the solebars. Also like the GWR cars they were well appointed inside with comfortable seating and were immediately popular. Soon afterwards, Córas lompair Éireann (CIÉ) south of the Irish border ordered a large fleet of almost identical vehicles that were delivered from 1952.

The Ulster Transport Authority moved quickly to convert locomotive-hauled carriages into its Multi-Engined DMU fleet (known as MEDs) for use on the Bangor and Larne suburban lines, beginning in 1953, thus completing Ireland's first wave of diesel railcar implementation. This was all done before the British Railways diesel multiple-unit programme had got seriously under way.

By 1952, British Railways had decided to try diesel railcars on both a heavily used inter-urban line and in rural areas. The first BR Derby and Metropolitan-Cammell products, introduced from 1954 and 1955 respectively, were of lightweight construction. Unlike the GWR and Irish main line cars, but reflecting the MED trains, the power cars on these British sets each had two bus-type diesel engines mounted horizontally under the vehicle floor driving through either hydraulic or mechanical transmissions. They proved their worth in two ways. They boosted carryings on the Leeds–Bradford route, and reduced costs usefully in the rural areas. The way was set for a large fleet of over 4,000 DMU vehicles to enter service on BR. Later variations included longer vehicles, suburban cars with multiple slam doors, heavy inter-city cars with buckeye couplers, and a small range of cars devoted to carrying parcels and mails. They used several different engine models and transmission types. Most, though not all, could multiple with other classes. They were built by several different companies to a variety of designs.

Hauling freight

Having had success with its MEDs on the Bangor and Larne commuter lines, the Ulster Transport Authority decided that converting carriages

into DMUs was the way forward for all its passenger services. In 1957 it launched its Multi-Purpose Diesels (MPDs). These were former UTA main line corridor coaches each fitted with one 275bhp turbocharged Leyland horizontal underfloor engine driving two axles through an hydraulic torque converter and gearbox transmission. They were geared for 90mph operation and put in service on the Belfast York Road to Londonderry Waterside route.

Uniquely, UTA intended to use the MPDs in pairs to move short container and works trains around the railway system. Thus UTA would eventually need no locomotives to work its main line services. A few non-corridor coaches were also converted to the same principle for local services out of Belfast York Road.

Exceptions

There were two major exceptions to this pattern of development. The Southern Region of BR had inherited the Southern Railway's extensive suburban and main line electrification system and wanted its new diesel vehicles to be similar to its electric multiple-units (EMUs). The British Railways Board agreed to this and so the SR built a range of diesel-electric multiple-units based on existing BR-style EMUs but with the power coming from diesel-electric power units instead of the conductor rail. The carriage frames, bodies, bogies and electric traction equipment were largely standard in design with existing BR mark 1-style EMUs. The DEMUs were solid, reliable vehicles, most of which had quite long life-spans.

Another type of diesel electric unit was built by Metro-Cammell to provide Pullman trains for the Manchester and Birmingham to London business services on alternative routes during the period of disruption when the west coast main line was being electrified. These units have a place in this book, if only because the former 'Midland Pullman' six-car

Among the longest living first-generation DMUs on BR were the Metro-Cammell Class 101 units. Two refurbished three-car sets arrive in Glasgow Central on a service from Largs in 1980. Author

sets, when transferred to the Western Region in 1966, were modified to work in multiple with each other to form a 12-car 'Bristol Pullman' service.

The author has thought long and hard whether to include the former British Rail high-speed diesel trains (HSTs) in this Compendium. Strictly speaking they are fixed formation train sets, not multiple-units. The HST power cars do not carry passengers, and are in principle Bo-Bo diesel-electric locomotives. A future Compendium is intended to group the HST power cars with other BR diesel locomotive designs.

More DEMUs

It was not long before engineers in Northern Ireland were extolling the virtues of the Southern Region DEMUs and wanting to follow this pattern for future new vehicles. A tentative step was taken in 1966–67 when English Electric delivered eight power car underframes and bogies fitted out with power units and traction equipment. UTA fitted these with new main line carriage bodies, upgraded some ex-NCC carriages to go with them as trailers, and formed them into six-car and three-car sets for the Londonderry line expresses and Belfast suburban services.

So successful were these that, when UTA's successor Northern Ireland Railways wanted to replace its worn out MEDs, MPDs and ex-GNR(I) railcars, it contracted BREL in Derby to built 22 brand new two-car and three-car DEMUs using the familiar English Electric equipment fitted in carriages based on BR's mark 2 coach design. These Class 80 sets entered service in the mid-1970s and were instantly successful. As a postscript to NIR's DEMU acquisitions, one must mention the nine 'Castle' class three-car DEMUs that BREL supplied to NIR using new bodies on second-hand BR mark 1 carriage underframes and fitted with power equipment taken from the older EE Derry line sets. This enabled NIR to eliminate its diesel hydraulic sets by 1981.

Second-generation fleets

At a time when the first-generation BR DMU fleet was ageing and when the country and BR itself were experiencing hard times financially, BR Research developed a four-wheeled vehicle design that was expected to ride acceptably well at speeds up to 75mph. The vehicle underframe and suspension design had originally been anticipated for use under high speed freight wagons, but the principle, using road-bus body components, was applied to a lightweight DMU fleet which became known as the 'Pacers'. At the time BR was not so much seeking popularity for these units as to save cash on essential fleet replacements.

Looking at experience abroad, each 'Pacer' car had a more powerful underfloor horizontal diesel engine driving a torque converter transmission. The 140-series units performed adequately, though their ride on jointed track left something to be desired. Later, a more conventional DMU replacement unit was developed by BR in the form of the 150-series which has formed the basis of most new designs ever since, at least up to the onset of privatisation of Britain's railways which took effect from 1995.

In 1993 in Éire, CIÉ began a slow process of providing two-car diesel-hydraulic multiple-units to replace short locomotive-hauled trains and to allow for some growth in passenger numbers. Batches of DMUs were ordered from Japan, then Alsthom in Spain, and then again Japan. These were followed by a large group of four-car suburban units from CAF in Spain that arrived just in time to pick up the surge in commuting caused by the 'Celtic tiger' economic expansion that started in the 1990s.

In 1990 BREL produced its first Class 165 wider-bodied DMUs for the Thames & Chiltern services of BR's Network SouthEast business.

Privatisation

When BR was privatised the new rolling stock leasing companies continued BR's policy of competitive tendering for new trains. Bombardier at Derby was successful in bidding for new DMUs for Midland Mainline services and in 1998 delivered the first of its long run of 100mph-capable 170-series 'Turbostar' units which were diesel versions of the company's 'Electrostar' EMUs.

The big revolution came when Virgin and Great Western wanted unit trains capable of 125mph, and Virgin wanted some with tilting bodies. The well-appointed Class 180 'Adelante' five-car sets appeared from Alstom's Metro-Cammell factory at Washwood Heath in 2000 for GW line services to Bristol and Hereford. In later years these went out of favour for reliability and non-compatibility reasons, and they were redeployed among open access and other train operators centred on the east coast main line.

From the same year, Bombardier provided two groups of 'Voyager' DEMUs with underfloor engines on all carriages and traction motors distributed along the train. Because some of these had to have body tilting, the narrower body profile necessary for tilt was employed as standard for the fleet. This led to critics complaining that the units were claustrophobic. Certainly the provision of three very large toilets and rather excessive (it seems to the author) anti-collision crush zones means that these units do not seat an economically optimum number of passengers. However, passengers have flocked to these speeded-up services and they are undoubtedly popular with many travellers.

Further versions of DEMUs using the same basic design layout as the 'Voyagers' were the 'Pioneers', four-car sets for Hull Trains, and the 'Meridians', originally four-car and nine-car sets for Midland Mainline. Their rather complicated story is told in this book.

In Ireland, NIR's policy for replacing the out-of-date and by then unreliable Class 80 DEMUs led to purchase of a batch of three-car diesel-hydraulic units from CAF in Spain. Arriving from 2002, their deployment caused an embarrassing increase in passengers such that not all the Class 80s could be spared for scrap and a further order for CAF units is in place as I write this Introduction.

Iarnród Éireann (Irish Rail, the rail component of CIÉ) has determined a policy of buying unit trains (multiple-unit or push-pull) for all its services. Current orders being delivered are for over 200 DMU vehicles from Rotem of Korea that have a top speed of 100mph and a high quality inter-city ambience. These are taking over all inter-city services radiating from Dublin other than those to Cork and Belfast which already have modern locomotive-hauled push-pull trains. The DMU is now king in Ireland!

Future builds

Apart from a few small batches of 'Turbostars', there are likely to be few new DMUs in the UK for some years. The British Government's new policy of progressive railway electrification (if it does not change) caused cancellation in 2010 of its plan to acquire 200 more DMUs. There would instead be a cascade of electric multiple-units into newly electrified areas, displacing existing DMUs for use elsewhere. This rather glib comment recognises nonetheless that there are capacity shortages on the railway at present that cannot adequately be addressed until this electrification begins to roll. As I write, we have a new coalition government and an urgent need for national expenditure to be drastically cut in order to rescue the national economy. Thankfully, the government has supported most railway development plans including electrification in the North-West and South-West (London-Bristol/Oxford/Cardiff). DMUs displaced from these schemes will ease overcrowding elsewhere.

THE FIRST DIESEL RAILCARS

County Donegal Railways Nos 7 and 8

The name Henry Forbes, the general manager of the three-feet gauge County Donegal Railways in Ireland, is historically synonymous with innovative use of internal combustion-engined railcars. By 1930 the railway already had six rail vehicles of this type. Four of these were petrol-driven railcars, and two were trailers which had both been converted from earlier railcars. That year, the railway had purchased a petrol railcar assembled at the GNR(I) works at Dundalk which had its body built by the coachbuilders O'Doherty of Strabane. This No 6 proved to be successful.

Two more similar vehicles followed in 1931 but these had 74-brake-horsepower Gardner 6L2 diesel engines, the same as used on the company's modern road buses. The first one delivered, No 7, was the first diesel railcar to operate in regular commercial service for an economic lifetime in the British Isles. This class had the engine and gearbox carried on a leading extension of the underframe with the carrying wheels well forward. The back of the passenger saloon rode on a conventional railway bogie. The diesel engine drove the wheels of the rear bogie.

These two vehicles were 32-seaters. The driver's seat and controls were at the front of the passenger saloon on the right-hand side in the direction of travel. There was an entrance doorway on the left side of the saloon for passengers; this was directly opposite the driver's position. Another passenger doorway was at the rear of the saloon on the right-hand side of the vehicle.

With a maximum speed of 43mph, Nos 7 and 8 proved to be useful railcars. They mainly worked services on the Glenties and Ballyshannon branch lines. These pioneer vehicles had a life of 18 years in traffic, being withdrawn in 1949. While this may be considered a short life for a rail vehicle, it was not unusual for a road bus, from which these vehicles were derived.

Below: No 8 was an identical vehicle, delivered one year later in 1932, and is seen also at Strabane with trailer No 2 that itself had been converted from an old petrol railcar of the same number. Note the fence across the platform behind the train, which restrained passengers while customs examinations took place. H. C. Casserley/IRRS

Class	CDR 7 and 8
Designed for	CDR
Introduced	1931
Built by	GNR(I) Dundalk, O'Doherty
Wheel arrgt	1-A1*
Layout	one driving position in saloon; unidirectional
Engine	Gardner 6L2, 74bhp
Transmission	4-speed mechanical gearbox and clutch
Weight in wo	7 tons
Max speed	43mph
Seats	32
Number built	2
CDR numbers	7, 8

* The axles on the rear bogie could be coupled by chains if adhesion conditions required it, making the wheel arrangement a temporary 1-B

Below: County Donegal Railways railcar No 7 was the first single railcar in the British Isles to be powered by a diesel engine. It ran for 18 years on branch line services, and pioneered the use of diesel railcars in the British Isles. It was photographed at the junction station at Strabane. H. Fayle/IRRS

County Donegal Railways purchased its diesel railcar No 10 second-hand from the Clogher Valley Railway when that railway closed in 1940; No 10 was thus the first second-hand sale of a diesel railcar in the British Isles! Its articulated layout is clear from this photograph of it on the turntable at Stranorlar in May 1959. Chris Gammell/Colour-Rail

The General Manager of the CDR, Henry Forbes, was a member of the Clogher Valley Railway's management committee and had been intrigued by that railway's first diesel railcar purchase from the works of Walker Brothers of Wigan. Purchased by the CVR in 1932, this vehicle had a relatively long-wheelbase power bogie at the front on which was mounted the driving cab, the diesel engine and the gearbox, together with the driving controls. The bogie wheels were coupled together by outside coupling rods just like on a steam locomotive. The passenger saloon seated 28 people; the saloon front rested on the power bogie behind its vertical centre line, the trailer bogie being pivoted under the rear of the saloon. When the CVR closed in 1941, this railcar was purchased by CDR.

Meanwhile, Mr Forbes quickly organised the purchase of two larger diesel railcars for the CDR from Walker Bros, Nos 12 and 14 arriving in 1934 and 1936 respectively. These had longer bodies seating 41 passengers. Like No 10 before them, they had half-width cabs, but future purchases, Nos 15 to 18, were given full-width cabs which improved their appearance. The final two diesel railcars were delivered to the CDR in 1950 and 1951. All the CDR's railcars frequently worked with trailers and could also haul small freight vehicles. In 1957, the author travelled in a train hauled by two such diesel railcars in tandem hauling three bogie carriages and three wagons and a brake van, totalling nine vehicles in all!

In the early 1950s, Córas Iompair Éireann delegated its dieselisation project for the West Clare section to Mr Leo Curran, son of the then CDR general manager, so it is no surprise that four diesel railcars of the same design as CDR No 20 were purchased from Walkers for that little railway. These railcars enabled the line to run a stay of execution until its closure in 1961, not long though and (with the exception of one body section) the cars were subsequently scrapped.

While the single-ended Gardner-Walker railcar principle was successful in Ireland, it was never taken up on the British mainland.

However, two of the Irish broad gauge (5ft 3in) railways acquired small numbers, more particularly the Great Northern Railway (Ireland). The GNR(I) had three such vehicles, Nos C^1 to C^3 which were used on stopping and branch line services, mainly in the border counties.

More promising was the construction in the late 1930s by the GNR(I) of four two-car sets, each with a power bogie in the middle, off which the passenger sections were articulated on the Gardner-Walker principle. These sets were for the Dublin suburban services out of Amiens Street station, including to the Howth branch line. Two also worked in Northern Ireland. Railcars D and E had three-axle power bogies with outside coupling rods, while Railcars F and G had two-axle power bogies. These lasted into the early 1960s.

A solitary diesel railcar was purchased by the Sligo Leitrim & Northern Counties Railway in 1947. Railcar B was the only Gardner-Walker single railcar to be duo-directional, having a small driving position at the rear of the passenger saloon, thus avoiding the need to turn at each journey's end. When that railway closed in 1957, Railcar B was sold to CIÉ.

The pioneering spirit of the County Donegal Railways proved beyond doubt that diesel railway vehicles could economically work passenger services, and had advantages over steam traction where traffic was relatively light. Other railways enthusiastically took up the general idea, but the single-ended Gardner-Walker articulated diesel railcars turned out to be a rather quaint blind alley that died out finally in the 1970s, after up to 40 years of nonetheless useful service.

Clogher Valley Railway Nos 1 and 2

The Clogher Valley Railway was a 37-miles-long, three-feet-gauge rural railway, laid mainly alongside roads, that linked the small town of Tynan, which had a station on the GNR(I) line between Clones and Armagh, and Maguiresbridge on the Clones–Enniskillen main line, passing through poor farmland on the way. In 1928 the two counties served by the loss-making line, Fermanagh and Tyrone, set up a management committee, one of whose members was Henry Forbes, at that time general manager of the County Donegal Railways.

In 1932, Walker Brothers of Wigan delivered to the CVR diesel railcar No 1. This broke new ground in the design of powered railcars. It set a principle that proved popular among some Irish narrow-gauge railways. The basic articulated form was as described on page 9 above. On this railcar the power bogie wheelbase was 6ft 9¼in with coupled wheels of 1ft 10in diameter. The trailer bogie had 2ft diameter wheels at 5ft centres. Other details are in the table.

A year later the CVR received its second diesel vehicle, No 2, this time designed for goods traffic. Again Walker's provided a similar power bogie but this time with a short open lorry body carried on its back and with no articulated section. Like No 1, this vehicle had standard centre-buffer couplings front and rear. This enabled it to haul freight trains, and

Class	CVR 1 and 2
Designed for	CVR
Introduced	1932; 1933*
Built by	GNR(I) Dundalk, Walker Bros
Wheel arrgt	B-2; B*
Layout	articulated; half-width cab; unidirectional
Engine	Gardner 6L2, 74bhp
Transmission	mechanical gearbox and clutch
Max speed	40mph
Seats	28
CVR Nos	1, 2*
CDRJC No	10

* Details asterisked are for No 2, which was not taken into CDRJC numbered stock.

also short passenger trains when other traction was not available. Both diesel vehicles were sold in 1941 to the County Donegal Railways, ex-CVR No 1 becoming CDR No 10. No 2 was used as a spare power bogie and did not enter CDR numbered stock. No 10 is preserved in the Ulster Folk and Transport Museum at Cultra.

Right: *Purchased new in 1931, the Clogher Valley Railway's articulated diesel railcar No 1 stands in the rain while working a passenger service. This car was later sold to the County Donegal Railways.* IRRS

Below: *The diesel rail lorry, No 2 on the CVR, was to the same basic design as the power bogie of No 1, but with a small open truck supported on the back of the bogie. It illustrates its ability to haul short trains in this picture taken on 12 May 1937 at Fivemiletown.* R. G. Jarvis/IRRS

Seeing the results of the Clogher Valley Railway's purchase of railcar No 1, Henry Forbes decided to introduce similar, but larger, cars to the CDRJC lines. The articulated type of railcar clearly offered more development potential than the older Nos 7 and 8. No 12 appeared in 1934 and looked similar to CVR No 1 but had a longer carriage body that seated 41 passengers. No 14 followed. Nos 15 to 18 were again similar but with full-width cabs giving them a more modern appearance. Nos 17 and 18 seated 43.

The railcars were used all over the CDRJC lines and covered the basic timetabled services. Steam-hauled passenger trains were now the exception, being employed for special workings and excursions during holidays. The railcars were capable of hauling trailer cars, and the later ones, being more powerful, could manage normal carriages which had greater capacity than the lightweight railcar trailers. A typical main line train would feature a Gardner-Walker railcar, a bogie carriage and one or two covered vans.

In hot weather, the engines tended to overheat and it was common for the bonnet side sheets, which were hinged at the top, to be swung and clipped upwards to enable more air to reach the engine compartment. Even like that the radiators could still boil over!

Liveried in an attractive cherry red and cream, the CDR diesel trains were a cheerful sight and, with their undoubted economy, needing just a driver and a guard (no fireman or secondman), they were instrumental in securing for over two decades the future of the railway.

Right: Railcar 12 of the CDRJC rolls into Donegal station from Strabane in August 1958. E. S. Russell/Colour-Rail

Below: Splendidly-restored Gardner-Walker diesel railcar No 18 with a full-width cab front stands outside the Foyle Valley Railway museum in Londonderry in May 2000. Behind it is railcar No 12. Author

Class	CDRJC 12 to 18
Designed for	CDRJC
Introduced	1934
Built by	GNR(I) Dundalk, Walker Bros
Wheel arrgt	B-2
Layout	articulated; half-width or full-width* cab; unidirectional
Engine	Gardner 6L2, 74bhp
	Gardner 6LW, 102bhp**
Transmission	mechanical gearbox and clutch
Weight in wo	12 tons
Max speed	40mph
Seats	41, 43
CDRJC Nos	12, 14–18
Number built	6

* Nos 15–18 had full-width cabs.
** Railcars 16–18 had 102bhp diesel engines.

County Donegal Railways Nos 19 and 20

The last diesel railcars delivered to the CDRJC were Nos 19 and 20, identical apart from their frontal livery treatment. These came in 1950 and 1951 and had a more modern appearance with flush cab fronts. They were also more powerful than the earlier railcars, with 102bhp engines. Nos 19 and 20 took up most of the passenger workings on the main line trains covering the full length from Strabane through to Donegal including the severe climbs from either direction over the Barnesmore Gap.

No 19 when delivered sported a grossly elaborate set of painted wings on its front. This was quickly replaced by an inverted cream triangle over its radiator grille. No 20 had cream front whiskers contained within beaded mouldings which were of quite pleasant aspect, and which remained throughout the vehicle's working life.

When the railway closed in 1960, railcars Nos 19 and 20 were sold as working vehicles to the Isle of Man Railway which was seeking some economy in working some services on its lighter-trafficked line from Douglas to Peel. The railcars were repainted all-over red, and were worked coupled back-to-back, the trailing car in either direction being set out of gear and with its engine shut down. This method of working lasted for several years.

Nos 19 and 20 still exist in IoMR stock and have been undergoing a prolonged restoration, hopefully eventually to return to traffic for special train workings.

Right: *Railcar 20 was the last to be delivered by Walker Brothers of Wigan to the CDRJC, arriving in 1951, and had a more modern appearance than the earlier cars. No 20 is seen at Donegal station in May 1957.* J. G. Dewing/Colour-Rail

Below: *After sale to the Isle of Man Railways in 1960, CDR railcars Nos 19 and 20 were used on the Douglas-Peel run, running back-to-back with the leading railcar towing the other dead. The pair is at Peel on 31 August 1962.* Author

Class	CDRJC 19 and 20
Designed for	CDRJC
Introduced	1950
Built by	GNR(I) Dundalk, Walker Bros
Wheel arrgt	B-2
Layout	articulated; unidirectional
Engine	Gardner 6LW, 102bhp
Transmission	mechanical gearbox and clutch
Weight in wo	11 tons 10cwt
Max speed	40mph
Seats	41
Number built	2
CDRJC Nos	19, 20
IoMR Nos	19, 20

CIÉ operated a number of three-feet-gauge railways, of which the West Clare had a long-term reputation as a ramshackle, uneconomic, unreliable railway (cf the well-known poem by Percy French). Leaving the Limerick–Galway line at Ennis, the WCR ran through the poor farmlands of County Clare and served two small towns on the Shannon estuary, the port of Kilrush and the seaside resort of Kilkee.

Such freight as there was – mixed, general goods manhandled from CIÉ broad gauge wagons at Ennis, and agricultural goods, plus some import/export freight through Kilrush – was unlikely to occupy more than one goods service in each direction each day. Nonetheless, as the traffic was fairly light, and the future of the railway depended on significant economies being made, CIÉ tried dieselisation as the only course to avoid complete closure.

Four Gardner-Walker diesel railcars were put into passenger service, working three return services to and from Ennis each day, with connections at Moyasta Junction at the far end for Kilrush and/or Kilkee. Each railcar hauled a passenger coach consisting of a bus body-derived carriage on an existing underframe and bogies. The railway was able to continue in operation from the railcars' introduction in 1952 until its closure in 1961. The railcars' power units were sent to Inchicore and later scrapped, but one carriage section survived for three decades, placed on an additional bogie and used for taking tourists on the 3ft-gauge peat bog railway around Bellacorick in north County Mayo, until Bord na Móna decided to discontinue that service.

CIÉ wanted the West Clare section to survive the economic downturn of the 1950s and ordered four railcars from Walker Brothers. This railcar is working a service from Ennis to Kilrush and is calling at Corofin in July 1957. The trailer vehicle was assembled by CIÉ using bus body components on an old carriage chassis. Author

Class	West Clare
Designed for	CDRJC*
Introduced	1952
Built by	CIÉ Inchicore, Walker Bros
Wheel arrgt	B-2
Layout	articulated; unidirectional
Engine	Gardner 6LW, 102bhp
Transmission	mechanical gearbox and clutch
Max speed	38.5mph
Seats	41
Weight in wo	11 tons 10cwt
Number built	4
CIÉ Nos	3386–3389**

* These vehicles were based on CDRJC railcars 19 and 20.
** Before commissioning, these vehicles were first numbered 286–289, then renumbered 386–389, before receiving their correct numbers.

GNR(I) C series

The GNR(I), being a part-owner of the County Donegal Railways, was clearly influenced by the positive effects of using diesel railcars on the narrow gauge railway. Having some lightly-used services of its own on the broad gauge, and having had promising results from its own railcars A and B (see page 24) the GNR(I) procured in 1934 a single-ended Gardner-Walker railcar, numbered C. As with the CDR railcars, the GNR(I) used a powered bogie supplied by Walker Bros in Wigan, and built the rest of railcar C in its own workshops at Dundalk. To keep the weight down to 14 tons, railcar C was built with a narrower-than-standard body width of just 8ft 0in. The body had a central passenger door on each side, with steps to near rail level to allow passenger access from low-level halts. Being unidirectional, the vehicle had to be turned at the end of each trip. To make best use of its interior for seating (it seated 50 people), a later addition was a small four-wheeled luggage truck that was coupled behind the railcar.

Two similar railcars, Nos C2 and C3, appeared in 1935, at which time railcar C was renumbered C1. The two new railcars were intended to be operated back-to-back as a two-car set, but with only the leading car powered, giving an inferior performance. As their initial use was on suburban workings between Dublin Amiens Street and Howth, this performance was not entirely satisfactory. Railcars C2 and C3 were soon split up, and towing small luggage vans joined No C1 on the lines radiating out of Enniskillen. In 1958 railcars C1 and C2 became part of

Class	C
Designed for	GNR(I)
Introduced	1934
Built by	GNR(I) Dundalk, Walker Bros
Wheel arrgt	B-2
Layout	articulated; unidirectional
Engine	Gardner 6LW, 96bhp
	Gardner 6LW, 102bhp*
Transmission	mechanical gearbox and clutch
Max speed	48mph
Seats	50 (C1), 52 (C2), 46 (C3)
Weight in wo	14 tons, 15 tons*
Number built	3
GNR(I) Nos	C1, C2, C3
UTA number	102**

NB: No C1 originally numbered C.
* Details refer to railcars C2 and C3.
** Railcar C3 (only) renumbered from 1958.

CIÉ's stock but saw little use thereafter and were withdrawn by 1961. C3 went to UTA, which listed it as No 102, but left it derelict at Belfast Adelaide until it was scrapped, also in 1961.

Above: *The Great Northern Railway (Ireland) tried three Walker railcars on its 5ft 3in gauge lines. This is the first one, No C1, leaving Enniskillen in July 1956 on a stopping service to Clones. Luggage was carried in the small wagon towed behind the railcar. The railcar was painted royal blue-and-cream.* Author

Right: *GNR(I) railcars C2 and C3 were coupled back-to-back to provide suburban services in the Belfast and Newry areas. Unlike No C1, these two had flat-backed bodies and gangway connections between them. The leading railcar towed the other one dead on each trip.* Sam Carse, courtesy of Barry and David Carse/IRRS

A major step forward came in 1936 with the construction of GNR(I) railcars D and E. These were each two-car units, with the passenger saloons articulated on a central three-axle power bogie. Following Walker principles, the wheels were coupled with external coupling rods and the engine was a Gardner diesel, this time the more powerful 6L3. The drive was through a Wilson four-speed epicyclic gearbox set up for automatic gear changing, a first on the GNR(I). The carriages were spacious, being built to the full width of 9ft 6in. Although a unit was 124ft long, the total weight was just 39½ tons. Nonetheless, 153bhp proved to be underpowered for the suburban duties intended for these sets, and in 1938 they moved north, working branch lines such as that between Goraghwood and Warrenpoint and later the UTA Bangor line.

In 1938 two more similar railcars, F and G, appeared from Dundalk Works for the Dublin suburban services. These two units had a shorter, two-axle power bogie with two Gardner 6LW engines giving 204bhp in all. Each engine drove one axle. Also, each engine had to be reversed manually; if one engine was forgotten, it was possible for one to pull against the other, though the author has not discovered whether that actually happened! Railcars F and G were 126ft long and normally worked the Howth branch.

In 1958 both railcar pairs were split between UTA and CIÉ. D went to UTA as its No 103, withdrawn in 1963. Railcar E was sold by CIÉ to

Class	GNR(I) two-car
Designed for	GNR(I)
Introduced	1938
Built by	GNR(I) Dundalk
Wheel arrgt	2-C-2; 2-AA-2*
Layout	articulated with central power bogie
Engine	Gardner 6L3, 153bhp;
	two Gardner 6LW, total 204bhp*
Transmission	four-speed Wilson epicyclic gearbox
Max speed	42mph; 48mph*
Seats	159; 164*
Weight in wo	39 tons 10cwt; 41 tons 10cwt*
Number built	2; 2*
GNR(I) Nos	D, E, F, G
UTA numbers	103 (D), 104 (F), 105 (G)

* Details refer to railcars F and G.

UTA in 1961 for spares. Railcar F became UTA No 104. It was scrapped in 1969 after some years with a contractor. CIÉ sold railcar G to UTA in 1962; as No 105 it replaced 103 on the Warrenpoint line, but was burned out in 1968.

Right: Ulster Transport Authority railcar No 103 was formerly GNR(I) railcar D. Still in base GNRB livery but renumbered, its three side-coupled wheelsets are clearly visible under the middle section which housed the diesel engines and gearboxes. Seen in service on the Warrenpoint line, it was withdrawn in 1963. Colour-Rail

Below: GNR(I) railcars F and G were more powerful, having two 102bhp diesel engines in their centre sections. This is railcar F at Dublin's Amiens Street station in August 1955. Note the four-wheeled power unit which had shaft drives to the axles. Ian Davidson/Colour-Rail

SL&NCR railcar B

In 1947, the impecunious Sligo Leitrim & Northern Counties Railway purchased a duo-directional diesel railcar from Walker Brothers of Wigan. This 5ft 3in gauge, 55ft-long vehicle followed the established Gardner-Walker layout except that it had a driving desk at the back of the passenger saloon, and so did not need to be turned at journey's end. Painted two-tone green, this railcar became the SL&NCR's most utilised passenger vehicle as it worked two return journeys each day between Sligo and Enniskillen. It was popular with passengers because its progress was free-running and almost vibration-free, and thus an improvement on the converted road buses or ancient carriages that worked other services.

When the SL&NCR closed in 1957, CIÉ bought railcar B, renumbered it 2509, and set it to work between Limerick and Nenagh. Later allocated to Waterford, railcar B was finally withdrawn in 1971. For many years it languished outside the depot at Mallow awaiting preservation but deteriorated severely. Railcar B is now safer under cover at Inchicore, still awaiting restoration and possible inclusion in a future Irish national railway museum.

Class	SL&NCR railcar B
Designed for	SL&NCR
Introduced	1947
Built by	Walker Bros
Wheel arrgt	B-2
Layout	articulated; duo-directional
Engine	Gardner 6LW, 102bhp
Transmission	fluid coupling and four-speed Wilson epicyclic gearbox
Max speed	42mph
Seats	59
Weight in wo	18 tons 12cwt
Number built	1
SL&NCR No	B
CIÉ number	2509

Above: *SL&NCR railcar B was the only 5ft 3in gauge Gardner-Walker single railcar to be duo-directional, having a driving position in the saloon at the non-powered end. The car was painted two-tone green with a white roof. It is seen entering Enniskillen station on the afternoon working from Sligo in July 1956.* Author

Right: *When working for CIÉ the former SL&NCR vehicle was painted black-white-and-tan and numbered 2509. It was glimpsed at Birdhill in 1963 on a local service to Limerick.* Author

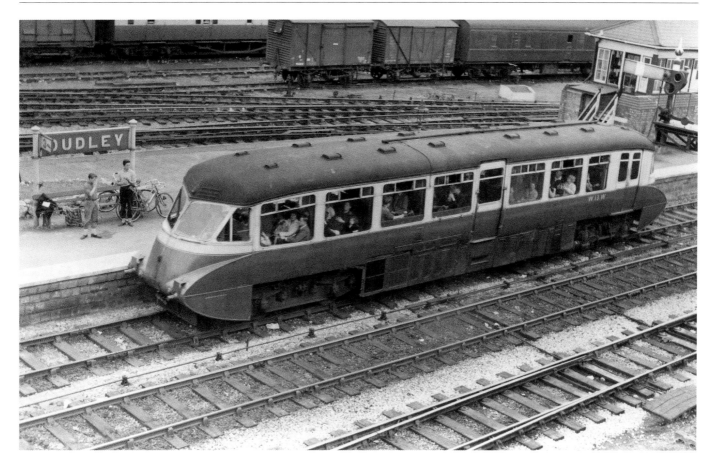

Between 1933 and 1942 the Great Western Railway received from AEC Ltd and Park Royal Coachworks Ltd, and also its own works at Swindon, a fleet of 38 bogie diesel railcars. The streamlined outline of railcar No 1 gained it immediate public admiration, but its meagre on-line performance with just one 125bhp diesel engine led to the rest of the fleet being built with two engines. Some were expected to run express services at up to 80mph; others were lower geared for suburban or stopping services.

There is no doubt that the original railcar No 1 was successful as so many more followed it in quick succession, though these were all subject to significant design improvements as experience was gained. The most significant change from No 2 onwards was the use of two AEC diesel engines instead of one. Satisfied as the GWR was with the acceleration from rest that one engine managed, the next few railcars had the second engine coupled directly to the wheels on the second bogie. The theory behind this strange arrangement was that the power from the second engine was really only needed when speed was above 40mph or so by which time its rate of rotation was sufficient to supplement the power from the main engine.

Needless to say, a diesel engine being constrained to run at speeds below its normal idling speed is not happy, nor indeed is it useful. GWR diesel railcars from No 7 upwards adopted the arrangement (today seen as sensible) of both engines driving through identical gearbox drive trains, one to each bogie. Railcar No 17 was built as a parcels car with wide side doors and no passenger accommodation.

As happened with the County Donegal Railway railcars, the popularity of the modern GWR diesel railcars led to the need to increase carrying capacity. Railcar No 18 therefore was designed so that the body sat on a more conventional carriage underframe that had standard buffers and drawhooks at each end, and was thus able to haul a normal carriage as a trailing load.

The GWR diesel railcars were innovative in many ways, including their streamlined styling which brought them public acclaim. No W13W arrives at Dudley in BR days on a working to Birmingham Snow Hill. J. B. Bucknall

This redesign again proved to be a successful development. All the later diesel railcars likewise embodied heavy underframes. They could thus not only haul trailing vehicles but could also couple to each other and run in tandem. From No 19 upwards railcar production was centred on Swindon Works. A redesign of the body shape resulted in a more angular appearance, easier to manufacture and not unattractive but probably less resonant of the 1930s in style. No 34 was another parcels car, this one being able to haul other vans as trailers.

The final development of the type came in 1941 and 1942 when Nos 35 to 38 entered service as single-ended cars, designed to couple back-to-back and be worked in multiple. When required, locomotive-hauled carriages could be coupled between two railcars to form a three- or four-car set, the carriage having to be wired up to the railcars to enable the diesel railcars to multiple with each other. These vehicles were effectively the progenitors of most British and Irish diesel multiple-units for the next few decades. One of these units was the first DMU ever seen by the author, on the Reading–Basingstoke line around 1944.

Because the later railcars used diesel oil-fired steam boilers to generate steam for heating, they could successfully operate with trailers or intermediate vehicles and provide steam heating as required. In the decades before the 1980s, most passenger carriages had individual belt driven generators to charge 24-volt dc lighting batteries, so no power was needed to be provided for this purpose by the railcars. The vacuum brake was provided on all these diesel railcars.

Most GWR diesel railcars survived into the days of British Railways, the last being withdrawn in the early 1960s. Three have survived into preservation.

GWR railcar No 1

In 1933, collaboration between the Great Western Railway, Hardy Motors Ltd of Southall (designers), AEC Ltd (power equipment) and Park Royal Coachworks Ltd produced the first of its bogie diesel railcars. Railcar No 1 was as much an experiment in the use of diesel traction as it was an astute exercise in marketing. Current wisdom was that the available power of current road vehicle diesel engines necessitated the adoption of light weight vehicles in order to get sufficient on-rail performance. GWR No 1 had a single AEC 125bhp diesel engine outside the underframe held vertically on an outrigger frame. The engine drove through a hydraulic coupling (fluid flywheel) and a four-gear pre-selector Wilson epicyclic gearbox. This drove a cardan shaft to a reversing gearbox; another shaft drove the nearest axle-end drive box. Another cardan shaft connected the two axle-end drives on that bogie. The vehicle body was oak-framed with lightweight aluminium sheeting. The railcar was not designed for hauling other rail vehicles, but had a pair of stub buffers and a concealed drawhook at each end for rescue purposes.

Internally the railcar was furnished to carry 69 third-class passengers. The exterior shape was fully streamlined, based on the results of wind-tunnel experiments, all part of the GWR's attempt to lessen the load on the diesel engine but also a way of impressing the general public. The streamlining pre-dated Gresley's work on the A4 Pacifics by two years.

The railcar was outshopped in full GWR passenger carriage livery of glossy brown-and-cream but with a white roof; the diesel engine exhausted near rail level making a white roof more practical, but risking some ingestion of exhaust fumes into the car when windows were open and the wind was in the wrong direction!

Class	GWR railcar 1
Designed for	GWR
Introduced	1933
Built by	AEC Ltd / Park Royal Coachworks Ltd
Wheel arrgt	B-2
Layout	duo-directional
Engine	AEC 6-cylinder diesel, 125bhp
Transmission	fluid coupling and four-speed Wilson epicyclic gearbox*
Max speed	63mph
Seats	69
Weight in wo	24 tons
Number built	1
GWR number	1
BR number	W1W

* One source quotes five-speed.

No 1 had a long career, being repainted by British Railways in its carmine red-and-cream colours. The author saw it working in the Reading area in the early 1950s, later numbered W1W, the prefix W indicating the region to which it was allocated, and the suffix W that it was a vehicle of GWR origin.

Drifting into Reading station on the Up main line in 1951 is AEC railcar No 1, by this time in BR ownership and painted in that organisation's carmine-and-cream colours and numbered W1. Author

Experience with GWR railcar No 1 led to the next development having two 130bhp AEC engines, one on each side of the underframe, each driving opposite end bogies. Railcars Nos 2 to 4 had a similar external appearance to No1 but had a top speed of 80mph, being intended for an express service between Birmingham Snow Hill and Cardiff. Internally these cars had low-density, comfortable seating with a small buffet facility.

The drive from one engine was similarly arranged to that on railcar No 1. Because the designers were convinced that only one engine was needed to accelerate the railcar from rest, the second engine was connected directly to its reversing gearbox without any change-speed gearbox in between. The throttle was arranged that full power could not be given to the second engine until the first engine was driving in top gear, when the extra power would be useful to enable the car to reach its maximum speed. Because it was not needed for initial acceleration, and thus would come into play mainly when speed was higher and output torque lower, the second diesel engine drove only one axle on its bogie. This arrangement worked, though modern diesel engine designers would frown at treating an engine in this way, particularly forcing it to run at speeds below its 450rpm idling speed down to a stop.

From car No 7, the second diesel engine drove through its own five-speed gearbox in what is now regarded as a conventional drive train layout. These later cars were given 70-seater layouts, except for Nos 10

Class	GWR railcars 2 to 17
Designed for	GWR
Introduced	1934
Built by	AEC Ltd / Park Royal Coachworks Ltd*
Wheel arrgt	B-A1 (Nos 2–6), B-B (7–17)
Layout	duo-directional
Engines	2 × AEC 6-cylinder diesels, 130bhp each
Transmission	2 × fluid couplings and five-speed Wilson epicyclic gearboxes**
Max speed	80mph
Seats	44 (2–4); 70 (Nos 5–9, 13–16); 63 (10–12); 0 (17)
Weight in wo	26 tons 4cwt (Nos 2–4); 25t 6cwt (5–7); 29t 18cwt (10–12); 28t 17cwt (17); 29t 10cwt (the rest)
Number built	16
GWR numbers	2–17
BR numbers	W2W–W17W

* Nos 5 to 7 bodies built by the Gloucester Railway Carriage & Wagon Company Ltd
** On Nos 2–6, second engine had direct drive to reversing gearbox

to 12 which included a toilet and seated 63. Railcar No 17 was a parcels car, intended to alleviate the need for some steam trains to carry parcels and thus speed up their station dwell times.

Railcar No 9 was burned out in 1945 and subsequently scrapped. No 2 was withdrawn by BR in 1953 following a collision. No 10 burned out in 1956. All AEC cars were condemned by the end of 1962. No 4 is preserved as part of the national collection.

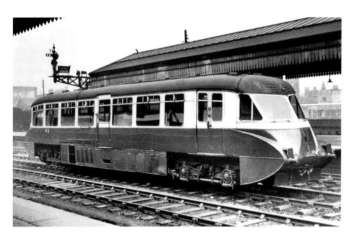

Left: *Streamlined GWR diesel railcar No W8 (the 'W' suffix not yet applied) calls at Birmingham Snow Hill in April 1954. This was one of the cars with two engines. The drive to the two axles in the nearest bogie is evident, the shaft gears driving the axle ends just outside the axleboxes.* Ian Allan library

Below: *One of the streamlined GWR railcars was a dedicated parcels car, No 17. It is seen passing through Birmingham Snow Hill station on 14 July 1955 liveried in BR's all-over carmine red with minimal black-and-cream lining and carrying its BR number W17W.* Author

Ordered in 1935, railcar 18 was a major step forward in that it was designed for haulage of conventional railway vehicles as trailers, in particular horseboxes between Newbury and Lambourn. Thus No 18 was given a more substantial underframe, longer-wheelbase bogies (8ft 6in instead of the former 7ft), and a full set of side buffers and standard screw couplings. A Clarkson steam generator was fitted that used the engine exhaust as its heat source. With end steam hoses, this facilitated steam heating of attached vehicles.

No 18 had a new, stronger final drive design. This replaced the worm gear previously used with a spiral bevel design suitable for the heavier loading required. This was a combined reversing and final drive gearbox. Between this and the Wilson gearbox was a speed-change box that could be manually changed when the railcar was stationary; this gave two maximum speeds, 80mph for express work and about 45mph when working stopping trains or towing heavier traffic.

No 18 retained the streamlined shape of the earlier cars, but with the side buffers protruding. The side valances that previously had hidden the bogies were eliminated. (In practice, on the earlier railcars the side valances were often left off to facilitate maintenance access.)

Class	GWR railcar 18
Designed for	GWR
Introduced	1937
Built by	AEC Ltd / Park Royal Coachworks Ltd
Wheel arrgt	B-B
Layout	duo-directional
Engines	2 × AEC 6-cylinder diesels, 130bhp each
Transmission	2 × fluid couplings and five-speed Wilson epicyclic gearboxes; also speed-change gearboxes
Max speed	80mph (45mph in low gear ratio)
Seats	49
Weight in wo	33 tons 12cwt
Number built	1
GWR number	18
BR number	W18W

GWR diesel railcar No 18 was a one-off, being the last streamlined one built, and the first to have conventional buffers and drawgear. It also sported vacuum and steam heat hose connections. Thus it was able to haul one or two parcels cars or additional carriages. Modern Transport/Ian Allan library

The next 16 diesel railcars were built by the GWR at its Swindon Works. These were very similar to No 18 in all features except the body shape. The cab ends which were clad in flat plates were quite angular in appearance. They had deep windscreens and side windows. Internally they were basically the same as the previous 70-seater vehicles.

Being fitted with side buffers and conventional drawhooks and screw couplings, they could haul passenger carriages when extra capacity was required. They could also heat these trailer vehicles using their diesel oil-fired steam generators.

No 34 of this batch was built as a second parcels car. Unlike parcels car No 17, No 34 was able to haul a number of vans and thus was a more useful vehicle.

In 1954 No 33 was rebuilt as a single-ended railcar to replace No 37 that had been destroyed by fire.

In GWR days these railcars carried the standard Great Western colours of brown-and-cream. From 1949 this was replaced by British Railways' carmine red-and-cream, or plain carmine in the case of the two parcels cars Nos 17 and 34. Some cars later received BR's light DMU green, based on the Southern Region's carriage stock green but lined with a white band below the windows. These Swindon-built cars were among the last survivors, but all were withdrawn by the early 1960s. Nos 20 and 22 survive in preservation.

Class	GWR railcars 19 to 34
Designed for	GWR
Introduced	1940
Built by	GWR Swindon
Wheel arrgt	B-B
Layout	duo-directional*
Engines	2 × AEC 6-cylinder diesels, 105bhp each
Transmission	2 × fluid couplings and five-speed Wilson epicyclic gearboxes**
Max speed	70mph**
Seats	48, 0***
Weight in wo	35 tons 13cwt; 34 tons 18cwt***
Number built	16
GWR numbers	19–34
BR numbers	W19W–W34W

* No 33 was converted in 1954 as a single-ended vehicle to replace No 37.

** Nos 19 and 20 had speed-change gearboxes giving 45mph maximum speed in low ratio.

*** No 34 was for carrying parcels.

Above: *The angular lines of former GWR railcars Nos 19 to 38 are demonstrated by No 22 in its preserved state at Didcot. Some side panels had been removed from the skirting while maintenance access was needed.* Author

Left: *Parcels car No 34 was able to haul additional vans to cope with extra demand as required. In BR carmine red, it was photographed at Southall in April 1953.* T. B. Owen/Colour-Rail

The last four of the Swindon-built railcars were designed to work as multiple pairs and thus had cabs at one end only. The other end of each railcar was blunt-ended with no driving cab and was fitted with a corridor connection. Other connections between the cars were for traction control, brakes and heating. The odd-numbered vehicles each contained a small buffet and toilets. Normally, railcar No 35 worked coupled to No 36; 37 worked with 38.

Early on in their careers, advantage was taken of the installed power of these railcars to convert a few main line passenger carriages to work with them. Inserted between each pair of railcars, a carriage that had through control connections would enable the leading car to control the traction in the rear car, the first example of a true multiple-unit in the UK. Indeed, these trains can be regarded as setting the example that most future diesel multiple-units would follow. The exception to this was the heating, which was by oil-fired steam generator. This method was used in some DMUs developed for Ireland (see next chapter), but did not prevail elsewhere in the UK.

In 1947, a fire destroyed railcar No 37. To replace it, in 1954 the GWR rebuilt No 33 as a single-ended car with corridor connection. Nos 35 and 36 also met a fiery end at Bristol in 1956.

There is a prototype for everything! One of BR's first diesel multiple units is formed by two of the Western Region's four single-ended diesel railcars, Nos W35W and W36W. The train is approaching Weymouth on a working from the Bristol line on 20 April 1954. The intermediate trailer car is an ordinary ex-GWR corridor coach with additional control connections. The two railcar sets were steam heated and vacuum braked. Author

Class	GWR railcars 35 to 38
Designed for	GWR
Introduced	1941
Built by	GWR Swindon
Wheel arrgt	B-B
Layout	single driving cab
Engines	2 × AEC 6-cylinder diesels, 105bhp each
Transmission	2 × fluid couplings and five-speed Wilson epicyclic gearboxes
Max speed	70mph
Seats	60 (35, 37); 44 + buffet (36, 38)
Weight in wo	36 tons 14cwt (35, 37); 37 tons 12cwt (36, 38)
Number built	4
GWR numbers	35–38*
BR numbers	W35W–W38W

* No 37 was withdrawn in 1949 after a 1947 fire and was replaced in 1954 by No 33.

Both the GNR(I) and the LMS(NCC) railways put small numbers of individual diesel railcars in service in the 1930s. While these might be regarded as something of an experiment, in reality they were used successfully for two or three decades on local stopping services either on main, secondary or branch lines. Each group is described on the following pages.

More important, however, is the way that the key DMU story switches back to Ireland in 1950 following the success of the GWR railcars described in Chapter 2. The Great Northern Railway (Ireland) had been impressed by their utility and availability, and could see advantages in using similar vehicles on its main lines. In 1950 the GNR(I) received delivery of the first of 20 single-ended diesel railcars, these being constructed by Park Royal Coachworks Ltd at Southall. Each railcar had two AEC 125bhp engines mounted vertically on outrigger frames, exactly as on the GWR railcars, of which these GNR(I) cars were a logical development. They were arranged as multiple-unit pairs, and GNR(I) converted existing main line corridor coaches to work with them, the normal formation being one trailer between each pair of railcars. One four-car set was assembled including a buffet car to work the nonstop 'Enterprise' service from Dublin to Belfast and back. The new trains looked smart in GNR(I)'s royal blue-and-cream livery.

CIÉ watched these trains with interest as it deliberated how it should proceed with its own dieselisation programme. It worked out that its most economical choice was to buy as many diesel railcar sets that it could fully utilise, and order diesel locomotives to cover all other passenger and non-passenger services. Thus CIÉ ordered a fleet of 60 diesel railcars from AEC and Park Royal that were almost identical to the Great Northern cars. Deliveries began in 1952. These units were formed variously into three- and four-car sets using mostly modern hauled carriages as trailers, and were liveried in light green. Eight-car express trains on the Dublin-Cork main line were sometimes made up with four power cars and included a buffet car. These railcars could be seen all over the CIÉ broad gauge system.

In parallel with these developments, the Ulster Transport Commission in Northern Ireland worked quickly to rid itself of steam on its suburban workings out of Belfast. The multi-engined diesel (MED) series of modern-looking DMUs utilised existing carriage underframes with new bodies built in the railway's own workshops at Duncrue Street, opposite York Road Works. AEC horizontal diesel engines under the floor were an innovation, but this time with hydraulic transmissions, something which

in practice had to be changed fairly quickly. They were built with sliding doors for passenger access, the first application of this modern feature on a significant DMU fleet in the British Isles and surprisingly not pursued elsewhere until the introduction of the BR 'Pacers' in the 1980s! However, UTA soon undermined this advantage and expanded the original three-car sets by inserting former locomotive-hauled slam-door suburban carriages. The MEDs took over all services on the Bangor line. When the extra slam-door carriages had been added to release some of the power cars, UTA was able to move a few MEDs to take over the Larne line as well.

In 1957 GNR(I)'s Dundalk Works built some more diesel railcars using underframes, bogies and BUT traction equipment supplied by AEC to the established pattern. Some of these vehicles were built as intermediate cars with half-width cabs at each end alongside corridor connections. Using these railcars, a smart eight-car corridor formation for the Belfast-based 'Enterprise' train was assembled.

The last of the new Irish DMUs covered by this chapter are the UTA multi-purpose diesels (MPDs). The first group of these was intended to modernise the Londonderry line services which in the late 1950s were still steam-hauled formations, normally of eight coaches on the expresses. The production of these new diesel trains followed UTA's established practice of utilising existing material as far as possible. Thus underframes and bogies were largely from former NCC carriages as were carriage bodies though considerably refurbished to a more modern, open interior. Each power car had a 275bhp horizontal diesel engine under the floor driving through hydraulic transmission to one bogie. A six-car Londonderry train would consist of four power cars and two trailers, possibly with a van or two in tow. At night, pairs of power cars coupled back-to-back would be used to haul short engineering trains or container flats to deliver freight consignments. Hence the title 'multi-purpose diesels'.

A small number of suburban carriages were also converted to the MPD principle, these retaining their basic body design with multiple slam doors and no gangways. They were used as two-car sets mainly on services on the Larne and Ballymena lines.

By the time all these DMUs had entered service they had successfully enabled the railways of Ireland to eliminate steam traction on passenger trains north of the border. Together with the second batch of General Motors diesel locomotives, CIÉ's diesel railcars had played a substantial role in the cessation of steam working in the republic by the end of 1963.

Naturally descended from the diesel railcars of the GWR, those of the Great Northern Railway of Ireland were comfortable vehicles that made a good impression on passengers when the first batch was introduced in 1951. This train is headed by three BUT cars of the 1957–58 batch and is entering Killester during Sunday wrong-line working, with the 10.20 Dublin – Belfast 'Enterprise' service in February 1959.
J. G. Dewing/Colour-Rail

GNR(I) railcars A and B

The Great Northern Railway (Ireland) foresaw uses for diesel railcars that not only reduced costs on sparsely-used local routes, but also could work main line stopping services so that express trains could miss stops and run to faster schedules.

Thus railcar A was designed with a relatively high power/weight ratio and a top speed of 50mph. Built at Dundalk Works in 1932, it was 40ft long and carried 32 passengers. Its 130bhp diesel engine drove both axles on the leading bogie through a fluid flywheel and mechanical gearbox. It was used on local services radiating from Portadown and on the Scarva–Banbridge line. The 2+2 seating layout was changed to 3+2 giving 50 seats, later reduced to 48 when one side entrance was widened from a single door to a double one. The AEC diesel engine was replaced later by a Gardner 6LW rated at 102bhp. The end radiator was replaced by one on the railcar roof.

Railcar A's construction was followed quickly by railcar B which was, unusually, a diesel-electric vehicle. Railcar B had a 120bhp Gleniffer diesel engine, mounted like No A on the bogie. Its generator fed a single traction motor on one bogie. The duty area was the same as railcar A. Railcar B was not used in passenger service during World War 2, and was de-engined in 1946 becoming carriage No 500. It was withdrawn in 1949.

However, in 1958 railcar A became UTA railcar No 101. It worked out of Londonderry Foyle Road to Strabane and Omagh. UTA painted it dark green with end wasp stripes. A collision in 1963 caused UTA to abandon its plan to preserve railcar 101 and it was withdrawn from capital stock in 1964. It later worked for a track-lifting contractor before being finally scrapped in 1970.

Class	GNR(I) railcars A and B
Designed for	GNR(I)
Introduced	1932
Built by	GNR(I) Dundalk
Wheel arrgt	B-2
Layout	duo-directional with two cabs
Engine	*AEC 6-cylinder diesel, 130bhp (A); Gleniffer diesel, 120bhp (B)
Transmission	fluid coupling and mechanical gearbox (A); Tilling Stevens dc generator and traction motor (B)
Max speed	50mph
Seats	32**
Weight in wo	18 tons 15cwt (A); 21 tons (B)
Number built	2
GNR(I) Nos	A-B
UTA number	101

*   Railcars A and B both had their engines replaced by Gardner 6LW of 102bhp.

**   Seating later increased to 50 on railcar A, then reduced to 48 when double-door added.

Top: GNR(I) railcar A was a diesel mechanical railcar that saw considerable use on local and branch line services over the years from its introduction in 1932. Its end radiator, seen here, was later replaced by one on the roof. IRRS

Right: Railcar B was different from A in that its drive was diesel-electric. This photograph was taken at Scarva and just shows the roof-mounted radiator at the far end of the car. IRRS

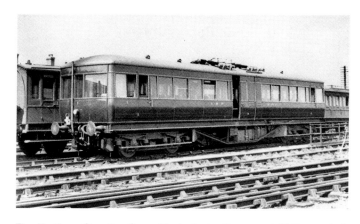

Class	LMS (NCC) railcars 1–4
Designed for	LMS (NCC)
Introduced	1933 (1), 1934 (2), 1935 (3, 4)
Built by	LMS (NCC) York Road
Wheel arrgt	B-2
Layout	duo-directional with two cabs*
Engine	2 × Leyland 6-cylinder diesels, each 125bhp
Transmission	2 × torque converters with direct drive above 25mph
Max speed	60mph
Seats	61, later 72 (1); 80 (2); 72 (3, 4)
Weight in wo	18 tons 15cwt (A); 21 tons (B)
Number built	4
NCC Nos	1–4
UTA numbers	1–4

* Railcars 2–4 had raised cabs in roof-line turrets, later removed from No 2.

The Northern Counties Committee's first railcar was initially a petrol-driven machine, but is included here because it was later re-engined with diesel engines.

No 1 was a conventional railway carriage, 54ft over the underframe with a wooden-framed body. It emerged from Belfast York Road Works in 1933. Under the centre of the floor were two Leyland horizontal petrol engines each of 130bhp, driving through Lysholm-Smith hydraulic torque converters. Above 25mph direct drive was engaged, bypassing the hydraulic transmission. The railcar had a top speed of 60mph, higher than any of its contemporaries. It had standard buffers and drawgear and could haul useful tail loads. No 1 received replacement diesel engines in 1947. In 1959 these were replaced with engines similar to those used on the UTA MED type of DMU. Railcar 1 was used mostly on stopping trains out of Belfast in the Larne and Ballymena directions. UTA withdrew it in 1965, and it still awaits restoration.

Railcars Nos 2 to 4 were built as diesel vehicles. No 2 was designed to be lightweight, coming out at 26 tons, but needed strengthening when the body flexed when lifted! Nos 3 and 4 weighed 28 tons each. The three initially sported small raised driving cabs, but No 2 was rebuilt by NCC on more conventional lines. It was withdrawn in 1954 and scrapped after 1966. A fire consumed much of railcar 3 in 1957. No 4 lasted in service until 1966, being scrapped three years later.

Two 17-ton bogie trailers for these railcars were built in 1934 as numbers 1 and 2. Trailer 1 became UTA carriage 544, withdrawn in 1968; No 2 became 545 and survived until 1978, lastly as a mess room.

Above: *LMS (Northern Counties Committee) diesel railcar No 1 was a successful experiment that led a useful and long life spanning 33 years. It had two vertical 125bhp diesel engines driving through hydraulic torque converters with direct drive over 25mph. Note the roof-mounted radiator. As pictured here it carried LMS crimson red livery.* L. Hyland/IRRS

Above: *LMS (NCC) railcar No 2 was built with raised driving cabs so that the driver could see when propelling a low-roofed trailer vehicle. It was later rebuilt with a more conventional layout.* H. Fayle/IRRS

Below: *NCC railcars 3 and 4 also had cabs that projected above roof level. This is smart-looking No 3 decked in LMS maroon and cream.* IRRS

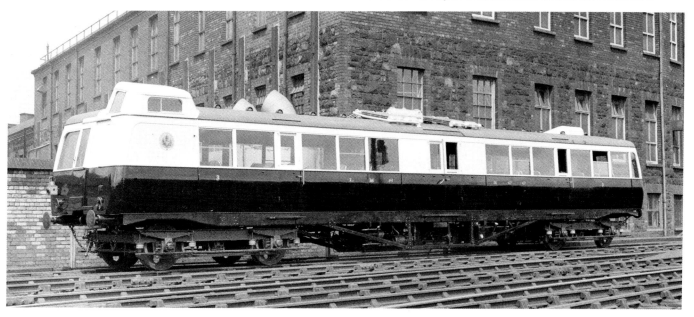

GNR(I) AEC and BUT railcars

Following the success of the GWR diesel railcars, the GNR(I) contracted AEC Motors Ltd to supply 20 similar vehicles for Irish service. These were assembled by Park Royal Coachworks Ltd in Southall, the cars being delivered in 1950 and 1951. AEC 125bhp diesel engines were fitted, two mounted on outrigger brackets under each railcar. The mechanical transmissions were fluid couplings driving Self-Changing Gears Ltd five-speed pre-selector gearboxes.

Dundalk Works rebuilt hauled carriages as intermediate trailers. These trains were self-contained, steam-heated units without provision for multiple-unit operation. At least one was formed as a four-car set for the Dublin–Belfast 'Enterprise' service. The rest were three-car units for main line and secondary services, particularly useful on the routes to Derry through Clones or Dungannon. Some worked as two-car units back-to-back, while one or two individual cars were used by UTA on local services with driving trailers (also converted steam stock).

In 1957 began delivery from Dundalk Works of 16 double-ended 'intermediate' diesel railcars, this time with BUT engines of 150bhp. They had four-speed gearboxes, also from SCG Ltd. The intermediate cars had a cab at each end with through end gangways of continental rubber-tube style. Eight single-cab railcars followed in 1958. The first four intermediate cars went into service on the Belfast–Dublin 'Enterprise' DMU roster with four rebuilt trailers between them.

The fleet was split between UTA and CIÉ in September 1958 and the CIÉ ones ventured onto other routes out of Dublin. Both countries' fleets had been withdrawn by the end of 1974.

Class	GNR(I) AEC and BUT* railcars
Designed for	GNR(I)
Introduced	1951; 1957*
Built by	Park Royal; GNR(I) Dundalk Works*
Wheel arrgt	B-B
Layout	duo-directional with one full-width cab**
Engine	2 × AEC 6-cylinder diesels, each 125bhp; 2 × BUT engines 150bhp each*
Transmission	2 × 5-speed SCG gearboxes and reversing final drives***
Max speed	70mph
Seats	44, 56*
Heating	diesel oil-fired steam generator
Weight in wo	38 tons 15cwt; 39t 10c (with boiler)
Number built	20; 24*
GNR(I) Nos	601–620; 701–716;* 901–908*
UTA numbers	111–120; 121–129;* 131–135*
CIÉ numbers	601N, 604N, 605N, 608N, 609N, 612N, 613N, 616N, 617N, 620N CIÉ also added the suffix 'N' to the car numbers of those BUT railcars it inherited

*   Details refer to BUT cars.
** BUT railcars 701–716 had half-width cabs and gangways at both ends.
*** The BUT cars had 4-speed gearboxes.

Above: *Ex-GNRB 600 series AEC railcar carrying the UTA number 112 (probably formerly GNRB 603) leaves Finaghy in May 1959.* J. G. Dewing/Colour-Rail

Top: *The first class interior of a GNR(I) diesel railcar had plush seating and plenty of space.* IRRS

Above: *Even the third class was comfortable and spacious.* IRRS

Left: *A pair of brand new BUT intermediate railcars leads the Up morning Belfast–Dublin 'Enterprise' service into Dublin Amiens Street station in July 1957. Two similar vehicles are at the rear. New end cars with full-width cabs would soon replace the outer railcars in this formation when completed at Dundalk Works.* Author

Class	CIÉ AEC railcars
Designed for	GNR(I)
Introduced	1952; 1956*
Built by	AEC/Park Royal
Wheel arrgt	B-B
Layout	duo-directional with one full-width cab**
Engine	2 × AEC 6-cylinder diesels, each 125bhp
Transmission	2 × 5-speed SCG gearboxes and reversing final drives with two-ratio gearboxes
Max speed	70mph/45mph
Seats	44 (2600–2647, 2660–2665), 48 (2648–2656); 56 (2657–2659)
Heating	diesel oil-fired steam generator
Weight in wo	38 tons 15cwt; 39t 10c (with boiler)
Number built	60; 6*
CIÉ numbers	2600–2659; 2660–2665*

*   Inchicore-built power cars.
** Inchicore railcars 2660–2665, and damaged cars 2666–2668 (new numbers) rebuilt as intermediate power cars.

CIÉ was quick to follow the GNR(I)'s lead and ordered 60 diesel railcars of the same design from AEC/Park Royal. Delivered between 1952 and 1954, these were painted in CIÉ's plain green livery. They were given centre trailers from the railway's fleet of modern (usually) corridor coaches. For main line work two power cars would work with two intermediate trailers with the two-ratio gearboxes set at 70mph maximum, fine for the less heavily graded routes such as most of the Dublin–Cork main line provided that drivers used all five gears. Some other routes only required three-car operation. For suburban and stopping train work, the lower ratio was selected. With a maximum speed of 45mph in low ratio, drivers could start a train in second gear.

CIÉ constructed a further six similar railcars with Bulleid-designed bodies in 1956. From 1961 these were converted to non-driving power cars. Three AEC railcars with accident damage were subsequently similarly rebuilt. Previously, an eight-car express might have three power cars at one end followed by four trailers and the other power car, thus denying access to the buffet car to passengers in the two odd railcars. The use of intermediate power cars resolved this anomaly.

CIÉ's railcar fleet spread all over the system. Cars 2657–2659 were transferred to the isolated Waterford–Tramore line to end the reign of steam there. In later years when more diesel locomotives were on hand, railcar withdrawals began. However, a need for push-pull working of

Dublin suburban trains caused CIÉ to de-engine many of the AEC cars. Rebuilt with hard plastic 'vandal-proof' seats, they became probably the least popular rail vehicles in the republic. Withdrawals accelerated when the DART electric service was introduced, and the Bray–Greystones push-pull shuttle was finally withdrawn in 1985. None is preserved.

Above left: When he was chief mechanical engineer of CIÉ, O. V. S. Bulleid had six additional railcars erected at Inchicore. These had a more angular cab front design but were otherwise clones of the Park Royal vehicles. This one leads a Dublin express being refuelled at Cork depot in July 1957. Author

Below: Two CIÉ AEC railcar sets, one four-car and one three-car, head south through Killiney en route from Dublin to Bray in May 1959. Two of the intermediate carriages are Inchicore loco-hauled products; the third vehicle in the train is a Park Royal outer-suburban built to a width of 10ft. J. G. Dewing/Colour-Rail

Leaving Belfast York Road terminus in summer 1963, a three-car MED unit with a slam-door intermediate trailer car heads towards the Larne line. The leading railcar has ribbed bodysides whereas the rear one has plain sides. For easier access to traction equipment, the side panels have been removed below solebar level. Author

Following the success of two prototypes (see page 118), UTA developed a fleet of suburban DMUs known as the 'multi-engined diesels' or MEDs for short. These were 60ft-long vehicles built at Belfast Duncrue Street Works in three batches. The first six, Nos 8–13, were conversions from prewar NCC main line open-third coaches. The second batch of 12 power cars, Nos 24–35, had new bodies on new LMS-design carriage underframes except that the last four of this batch had integral bodies and underframes. The final batch of 10 cars, Nos 14–23, were conversions from older NCC carriages dating from the 1920s. Fourteen trailer vehicles were built new with integral bodies, thus enabling 14 three-car DMU sets to be formed.

All cars had power-operated passenger sliding doors, a first in the UK for a DMU fleet. The MEDs had air brakes operated by electro-pneumatic valves for simultaneous action along the train, and engine waste-heat heating. They were fitted for multiple-unit working.

The MED power cars each had two Leyland 125bhp horizontal diesel engines driving through hydraulic torque converters and auxiliary gearboxes. Above a certain speed direct drive was initiated. From 1956 new BUT engines of 165bhp replaced the originals. Each power car pair could now work with two trailers; 12 prewar slam-door suburban vehicles were adapted to work within the MED sets, releasing some sets to work on the Larne line. The hydraulic transmission was later replaced by Wilson four-speed gearboxes. Later, five trailers were converted into driving trailers, though three of these lost their controls when they were used to fit additional cabs to railcars 24, 26 and 28 to make them double-

Class	UTA MED DMUs
Designed for	UTA
Introduced	1952
Built by	UTA Duncrue Street, Belfast
Wheel arrgt	1A-A1 (power cars)
Layout	duo-directional with one full-width cab*
Engines	2 × Leyland O/600 125bhp diesel engines; replaced from 1956 by 2 × Leyland O/680 6-cylinder diesels, each 165bhp
Transmissions	2 × Lysholm-Smith torque converters; replaced from 1966 by 2 × Wilson 4-speed gearboxes; two-ratio gearboxes; reversing final drives
Max speed	55mph/73mph**
Seats	52 (brake cars); 60; 78 (trailers)
Heating	Engine waste-heat (power cars); coke stove (trailer cars)***
Weight in wo	36 tons (8–31); 34 tons (32–35); 26 tons (trailers)
Number built	14 × 3-car sets
UTA numbers	8–35 (power cars); 201–214 (trailers)#
Post-1959 Nos	8–35 (power cars); 501–514 (trailers)##

*   Nos 12 and 13 were built as intermediate cars with no cabs but were soon rebuilt with cabs. Nos 24, 26 and 28 became two-cab vehicles in 1961 using equipment from driving trailers 505–507.
**   Normally set at 55mph for suburban work.
*** Replaced by paraffin Smith's heater.
\#   Trailers 204–209 converted to driving trailers 1957–1958.
\#\# Driving equipment removed from 505–507, 1961. Trailers 508, 511–513 were converted to parcels cars with no windows and manually-operated double doors around 1975, becoming Nos 631–634.

ended single units. All the MEDs were scrapped by the early 1980s (some by being tipped into a deep, flooded quarry) and none is preserved.

UTA wanted to replace the steam-hauled expresses on the Belfast–Antrim–Londonderry route by diesel railcars capable of fast running. The company also proposed that these should, in multiple, be capable of hauling the short freight trains envisaged for the future. Thus was born the 'multi-purpose-diesel' concept (MPD). Each power car had an underfloor 275bhp turbocharged new version of the Leyland Albion 0/900 six-cylinder horizontal diesel engine. This drove a Schneider single-stage torque converter coupled to an automatic four-speed duo-directional gearbox. From this a cardan shaft drove the nearest wheelset on the trailing bogie, a further shaft coupling both axles together. The railcars had air brakes and waste engine heat for carriage warming.

The lack of investment cash available led UTA to rebuild existing carriages, starting in 1957 with some modern coaches that had been delivered in 1951 for the Derry road and which formed railcars Nos 36–45. Nos 46–53 were converted from suburban non-corridor coaches, though these were rebuilt with corridor connections in 1968–1970. Then followed more conversions in main line style, Nos 54–62. The last three conversions, Nos 63–65 in 1961, were turned out as double-cab vehicles. Eighteen trailer car conversions were also carried out, including three buffet cars. Six of these trailers were modified as driving trailers in 1969–1971.

The MPDs were normally kept on the NCC routes to which they were most suited due to their good hill-climbing and their ability to run at 80mph+ speeds. Their reliability was always a problem, not helped by having to haul heavy Dublin–Londonderry container trains which strained the engines.

Class	UTA MPD DMUs
Designed for	UTA
Introduced	1957
Built by	UTA Duncrue Street, Belfast
Wheel arrgt	2-B (power cars)
Layout	duo-directional with one full-width cab
Engine	Leyland 0/900 275bhp 6-cylinder diesel; replaced from 1964 by AEC A1100H naturally-aspirated diesel, 260bhp (12 cars); Rolls-Royce C6/TFHL 275bhp diesel (17 cars)
Transmission	Schneider single-stage torque converter, reversing gearbox, SCG R14 four-speed gearbox
Max speed	90mph*
Seats	various
Heating	Engine waste-heat (power cars); oil-fired air heaters (trailers)
Weight in wo	39 tons to 42 tons (power cars); 30 tons approx. (trailers)
Number built	30 (power cars); 18 (trailers)
UTA numbers	36–65 (power cars); 529–543 (trailers); 548–550 (buffet cars)

* Officially there was no stated top speed for MPDs. The UTA officially limited ex-NCC routes to 70mph.

Four power cars were burned out and four succumbed to crash damage. Withdrawal of the remaining 22 was completed by 1983.

Above: *An express train of four Multi-Purpose Diesel express vehicles flanking a Stanier carriage intermediate trailer awaits departure for Belfast York Road from Londonderry Waterside station on 20 August 1958.* IRRS

Left: *A two-car suburban MPD unit approaches Belfast York Road from Larne in 1963.* Author

CHAPTER 4: BR LOW-DENSITY DMUS

The new DMUs that spread across British Railways in the 1950s were popular among travellers and undoubtedly staved off some line closures for a few years. A happy crowd alights at Mildenhall in June 1962. The Wickham-built DMU shows off its blue-square coupling code by the two small squares painted above its buffers. Colour-Rail

To reduce costs on urban and rural railways, British Railways specified initially some lightweight DMUs that would have low-density seating of road bus style. Maximum speed was to be 70mph, and the power cars would each have two underfloor bus-type diesel engines set horizontally, driving separate inner axles through hydraulic or mechanical transmissions. The first two manufacturers to design and produce these were BR's own Derby Works and the private company Metro-Cammell of Birmingham. The first 'lightweights' duly appeared in 1954 and 1955 respectively and became immediately popular among the travelling public through their cleanliness and modern appearance.

Following on from BR's first aluminium-bodied offerings, an all-steel design was thought to offer cheaper manufacture. The first of these were two-car power-plus-trailer sets for Lincolnshire services. Being significantly heavier, these proved to be underpowered and were re-engined with 230bhp Leyland Albion engines, a type used subsequently on other DMUs that needed higher performance. On the other hand, a class of three-car sets of similar layout working in Scotland coped adequately with the original 150bhp engines, albeit with four of them.

Once the concept had been proven, other manufacturers were engaged to design and build DMUs. These sets emerged to be of varying designs, all aiming at reasonable weight. Companies such as Park Royal Coachworks Ltd, the Gloucester Carriage & Wagon Company, and Wickham Ltd produced small batches of useful two-car units but no further were ordered. Instead, Metro-Cammell, the Birmingham Railway Carriage & Wagon Company and Cravens Ltd received follow-on orders, as did BR's own Derby workshops.

A general principle was the use of electro-pneumatic (EP) valves to operate the transmission equipment: gear changing, throttle settings, reversing dogs, were all operated by EP valves which were electrically-driven and which opened air valves to shift the mechanical parts of the equipment. This multiplicity of EP valves was surprisingly reliable when one considers the frequent use to which they were subjected. For example, a three-car DMU working a service from Glasgow to Ayr, stopping at 11 stations, would require a minimum of 480 EP valve operations; a typical day's work could entail on one DMU set some 5,280 EP valve operations!

Low-density cars were generally used on inter-urban and secondary line services all over the BR system with the exception of the Southern Region (but see Chapter 8). The body layouts were all very similar, comprising saloons entered through slam doors spaced out on each side of the vehicle.

There were extra doors at guards' compartments and a driver's door each side of the cab. Some vehicles included a short first-class saloon. This was normally located immediately behind the driving cab. A second-class saloon at the other end of the unit usually had a similar view forward.

Seating in these cars was of lightweight, steel-framed construction with low backs and sponge rubber or similar seat squabs and backs. In first-class saloons seating was in 2+2 format, and in second class it was normally 2+3. Side windows were wide, and had top sliding glass ventilators.

These DMUs were almost all arranged to multiple together, having a 'blue square' coupling code. Initially, only the original lightweight units were unable to multiple with the rest. The early lightweights, all numbered in the 79XXX series, were relatively short-lived and were the first BR DMUs to be withdrawn as the Beeching plan progressed and secondary and branch lines closed.

Exceptionally, a group of Cravens two-car units had single Rolls-Royce 238bhp engines under each car, the units being arranged as power-twins. These drove through hydraulic torque converters and were intended to provide good performance on the hilly routes around east Lancashire. Their Achilles' heel was the fuel tank design which enveloped a space through which the drive shaft rotated. On rare occasions when a shaft became disconnected, the resultant damage caused fires to ignite. This fleet was consequently withdrawn ahead of its contemporaries. The Metro-Cammell 101 series lasted longest, some of them working into the 21st century before finally being displaced by modern DMUs. Examples of low-density DMUs from all manufactures are preserved, though not all variations.

Although all first-generation BR DMUs, that is those built between 1954 and 1963 inclusively, were numbered with letter prefixes showing the region to which each car was allocated (ie, E for Eastern, etc), the many reallocations that took place during their lives make it impractical for these prefixes to be shown in the essentially compact tabular information in this book.

Class	Derby 'lightweight' DMUs
Designed for	BR
Introduced	1954
Built by	BR Derby
Wheel arrgt	1A-A1 (power cars)
Layout	duo-directional with one full-width cab
Engines	2 × Leyland 0/600 125bhp diesel engines;* 2 × AEC 6-cylinder 150bhp diesels
Transmissions	2 × Lysholm-Smith torque converters;* 2 × Wilson 4-speed gearboxes; reversing final drives
Max speed	62mph*/70mph
Coupling code	red triangle,* yellow diamond
Seats	52–79 (power cars); 45–69 (trailers)
Heating	Smith's oil-fired warm air heaters
Underframe	57ft
Weight in wo	27 tons (power cars); 20 tons (trailers)
Number built	16;* 203
BR numbers	79000–7,* 79500–7,* 79008–46, 79118–154, 79169–181, 79184–193, 79508–512, 79900–1** (power cars); 79250–262, 79325–329, 79400–404, 79600–625, 79633–635, 79639–684 (trailers)

* Original West Yorkshire power-twins.
** Two-cab single vehicles.

The initial series production DMUs for BR were two groups of 'lightweight' two-car sets. The first group was a batch of eight two-car sets for the hilly Leeds–Bradford route. To provide quick acceleration and good hill-climbing ability yet enable a 62mph top speed, each unit was formed of two power cars, each of which had a pair of Leyland six-cylinder horizontal diesel engines of 125bhp driving through Lysholm-Smith torque converter transmission. This arrangement was very similar to that first used on the UTA MED DMUs in Northern Ireland, described on page 28.

The bodies were built of aluminium to keep the weight down, and were insulated with sprayed asbestos. The Gresham & Craven quick-release vacuum brake had previously been used on the GNR(I) BUT railcars (page 26).

As Lysholm-Smith torque converters were imminently going out of production due to the road bus industry moving to mechanical drives, the next Derby-built DMUs had hydraulic couplings (sometime called fluid flywheels) driving Wilson four-speed gearboxes. This fleet had AEC 150bhp diesel engines. These trains were two-car power-trailer units for rural services in Cumberland and eastern England. This design continued in production until there were 203 vehicles in operation, arranged in two-car and four-car sets and as a few single vehicles with two cabs. All the BR 'lightweights' had 57ft-long underframes and most were geared for 70mph maximum speed.

One two-car unit was used as the basis for the experimental battery-electric unit that worked for a time on the Ballater branch in Scotland.

As the railway closures of the 1950s and 1960s proceeded, some DMUs became surplus and the earliest units described on this and the next page were the first to be withdrawn. Individual vehicles survived to be modified for specific departmental duties, which is how two Derby 'lightweights' became treasured preserved examples of BR's first venture into DMU production.

Above left: A Derby 'lightweight' two-car unit stands at Stratford depot, Eastern Region, on 11 May 1957. The nearest vehicle is the driving trailer. The prominent case below the solebar is the battery box. Author

Left: The two double-cab single-car Derby 'lightweights' coupled in multiple wait at the terminus at Buckingham. Colour-Rail

Metro-Cammell 'lightweight' DMUs

Class	Metro-Cammell 'lightweight' DMUs
Designed for	BR
Introduced	1956
Built by	Metropolitan-Cammell
Wheel arrgt	1A-A1 (power cars)
Layout	duo-directional with one full-width cab
Engines	2 × AEC 6-cylinder 150bhp diesels
Transmissions	2 × Wilson 4-speed gearboxes; reversing final drives
Max speed	70mph
Coupling code	yellow diamond
Seats	57/53* (power cars); 71/65* (trailers)
Heating	Smith's oil-fired warm air heaters
Underframe	57ft
Weight in wo	27 tons (power cars); 25 tons (trailers)
Number built	36 two-car sets
BR numbers	79047–75, 79076–82* (power cars); 79263–291, 79500–507* (trailers)

* East Lancashire units.

Once BR management had realised the success of relatively high-performance DMUs in attracting new traffic, the policy developed that would lead to over 4,100 DMU vehicles being produced, mainly in the 1950s and up to 1963. Such quantity production was beyond the capacity of BR's workshops. Tenders thus went out to all possible companies in the UK that conceivably could build railway carriages, but not before Metro-Cammell had produced a small fleet of 36 'lightweight' twins. These were specially designed to reduce weight to the minimum and successfully at that because each power car weighed only 27 tons (as did the first Derby vehicles) and the trailers 25 tons (against Derby's minimum of 20 tons).

The Metro-Cammell 'lightweights' had AEC 150bhp engines driving through what was to become the standard fluid flywheel and Wilson four-speed gearbox, with a final drive on the inner axle of each bogie fitted with reversing dogs.

Twenty-nine of these two-car sets worked in East Anglia, with the other seven working in Lancashire on the Bury–Bacup line and other services. Like the Derby 'lightweights' described on page 31, these early DMUs were withdrawn during the post-Beeching cull of non-standard types. None is preserved.

Above left: The interior of a third class saloon in one of the units used on the Bury to Bacup line in Lancashire shows the light and easy-to-clean interior of many of the early types of BR DMUs. Ian Allan library

Below: Met-Cam 'lightweight' E79066 leads a driving trailer at Aldeburgh on 10 September 1966. These units were among the first to be withdrawn after the Beeching cuts had closed many branch lines. Colour-Rail

Class	114 Derby DMUs
Designed for	BR
Introduced	1955
Built by	BR Derby
Wheel arrgt	1A-A1 (power cars)
Layout	duo-directional with one full-width cab
Engines	2 × Leyland Albion 6-cylinder 230bhp diesels; 2 x Rolls-Royce 8-cylinder 238bhp diesels*
Transmissions	2 × 4-speed gearboxes; 2 × hydraulic torque converters;* 2 × automatic SCG gearboxes;** reversing final drives
Max speed	70mph
Coupling code	blue square
Seats	62 (power cars); 74 (trailers)
Heating	Smith's oil-fired warm air heaters
Underframe	63ft 6in
Weight in wo	36 tons (power cars); 29 tons (trailers)
Number built	50 two-car sets
BR numbers***	50000–49 (power cars); 56000–49 (trailers)

*   No 50000.
**   No 50049.
*** In 1983, vehicles in the 50XXX series were renumbered into the 53XXX series with the final three digits unchanged; trailers in the 56XXX series became the 54XXX series. This was to avoid a clash with locomotive numbers in the TOPS computer system.

The first of the Derby Works-built 'heavyweight' DMUs emerged in 1955. The carriage bodies were of normal steel construction as used on the BR mark 1 carriages except that the body profile did not follow the curved sides of the mark 1s, nor indeed that of the 'lightweight' DMUs, but had flat sides inclined slightly inwards towards the cantrail, and a pronounced tumblehome at the bottom edge above the solebar. Possibly learning from the Metro-Cammell style, these new units had sloping cab fronts, a little less stark perhaps than that of the original Derby DMUs. The steel-bodied units initially had BUT (Leyland) 150bhp diesel engines driving through standard Wilson four-speed gearboxes.

A two-car unit weighed 65 tons, compared with the 47 tons of the Derby-built power-trailer 'lightweight' units. It was soon evident that the power/weight ratio of 4.6bhp/ton was no match for the 6.4bhp/ton of the Cumberland sets, nor the 9.3bhp/ton of the West Yorkshire power-twins. The M&EE department quickly decided to replace the 150bhp engines and gearboxes with more powerful equipment, namely the Leyland Albion 0/900 engines matched with more robust gearboxes. As an experiment, car No E50000 had two Rolls-Royce 238bhp engines driving hydraulic torque converters; it was withdrawn as non-standard in 1967. Also, No 50049 ran with a pair of automatic gearboxes supplied by Self-Changing Gears Ltd. For most of their lives this fleet of robust 50 two-car units was based at Lincoln depot. Moved to Tyseley in 1987, the whole class had gone by 1992. Towards the end of their lives five two-

car sets had been converted for use as parcels DMUs (see Chapter 7, page 62), two of which later went into departmental service. Two power cars and three driving trailers are preserved.

Above left: *The first 'heavyweight' DMUs were the E50000 series with longer underframes and steel bodies. Based for much of their lives at Lincoln depot, this picture shows a unit leaving Lincoln Central for Grantham on 21 May 1960. Trailer car E56047 is nearest the camera.* Author

Below: *Nearer the end of their lives, '114s' allocated to Tyseley depot worked outer-suburban services around the West Midlands. This one is leaving Hednesford on a free 'open day' service on the Sunday before the branch from Walsall was reopened on 10 April 1989.* Author

BR Class 107 DMUs

For completeness, though not in chronological order since they appeared as late as 1960, it is appropriate to detail the other two classes of low-density DMU that Derby Works produced before venturing into the offerings of private-sector companies. Indeed, the last such design produced at Derby was for the Scottish Region and was a group of 26 three-car sets for outer suburban services such as those to Largs, Kilmacolm, Paisley Canal and Ayr. On 58ft underframes, they were of steel construction and looked similar to the longer-underframe Class 114 units. With four standard 150bhp BUT engines and an all-up weight of 97 tons, a three-car unit had 6.1bhp/ton power/weight ratio which was fine for the outer suburban work they had to do in carrying commuters and holidaymakers between Glasgow and the Ayrshire coast.

Like all BR's low-density units, the end cars had a clear view through the driving cab which was popular with passengers.

For most of their lives, the '107s' were based at Hamilton depot, an odd arrangement following that depot's isolation from the DMU working area by the 1960s electrification of the Hamilton circle lines. The '107s'' daily mileage was therefore increased by empty stock workings to and from their home depot. For operating purposes they were fuelled and cleaned at Corkerhill in south Glasgow. It was only in the 21st century that Corkerhill depot gained a proper maintenance facility, by which time the erstwhile '107s' had long been withdrawn, the last going in 1992. They had spent virtually their whole lifespan in Scotland, apart from one intermediate trailer which for some reason ended up working on the London Midland Region. Ten '107' power cars and one trailer vehicle are listed as preserved.

Class	107 Derby DMUs
Designed for	BR
Introduced	1960
Built by	BR Derby
Wheel arrgt	1A-A1 (power cars)
Layout	duo-directional with one full-width cab
Engines	2 × BUT 6-cylinder 150bhp diesels
Transmissions	2 × 4-speed Wilson gearboxes; reversing final drives
Max speed	70mph
Coupling code	blue square
Seats	52/65 (power cars); 71 (trailers)
Heating	Smith's oil-fired warm air heaters
Underframe	58ft
Weight in wo	35 tons (power cars); 28 tons (trailers)
Number built	26 three-car sets
BR numbers	51985–52036 (power cars); 59782–59807 (trailers).

Class 107 three-car unit No 107 439 leaves Glasgow Central on a working to East Kilbride. The key recognition feature of this steel-bodied class, which was almost exclusively used in Scotland, was that the '107s' were the only class of short-underframe BR-designed low-density DMUs which did not have a curved bodyside profile; they were flat-sided above waist level and had a pronounced tumblehome below, a feature they shared with the longer-underframe Class 114s. From the late 1980s, most plain rail blue DMUs were repainted blue-and-grey which enhanced their appearance. The class began with four-digit route indicators, but these were later blanked off, as seen here. Author

In 1959, BR Derby embarked on its second design of lightweight DMU, similar in its curved body profile to the original 'lightweights' but with the more modern cab front that had become standard well before their introduction in 1958. Also on 57ft underframes, these vehicles were used widely on the London Midland, Eastern and North-Eastern Regions in formations ranging from two-car to four-car sets.

Externally they sported two-digit train indicator panels on the cab fronts (later blanked off) and destination blinds above the centre cab windscreen. Later units were built with roof-level four-digit train describer code indicators above the cab windscreens.

In common with other longer-lived classes, the '108s' went through BR's refurbishment programme in the 1980s. This replaced the old tungsten interior lighting with more modern fluorescent strips behind diffusers, brightened up the interior walls with coloured panels, blessed them with new seat moquette, and with an off-white livery instead of rail blue. Later they became blue-and-grey, though many received the various colours of the Passenger Transport Executives within whose areas they worked.

Also in common with all the other low-density classes of DMUs, the '108s' had standard side buffers and screw couplings throughout, and were gangwayed within sets with long concertina-type connections. They were of the 'blue square' coupling code which meant that they could couple with most other DMU types, other than the early 'lightweights' and Inter-City

Class	108 Derby DMUs
Designed for	BR
Introduced	1959
Built by	BR Derby
Wheel arrgt	1A-A1 (power cars)
Layout	duo-directional with one full-width cab
Engines	2 × Leyland 6-cylinder 150bhp diesels
Transmissions	2 × 4-speed Wilson gearboxes; reversing final drives
Max speed	70mph
Coupling code	blue square
Seats	52/65 (power cars); 50/68 (trailers)
Heating	Smith's oil-fired warm air heaters; later supplemented by waste engine heat
Underframe	57ft
Weight in wo	29 tons (power cars); 22 tons (trailers)
Number built	329 vehicles
BR numbers*	50599–50646, 50924–35, 50938–87, 51416–24, 51561–72, 51901–50, 52037–65 (power cars); 56190–215, 56221–79, 56404–504, 59245–50, 59380–90 (trailers)

* In 1983, vehicles in the 50XXX series were renumbered into the 53XXX series with the final three digits unchanged; trailers in the 56XXX series became the 54XXX series.

and other higher-powered units. In later life the power cars were modified to heat the saloons using waste heat from the engines (note that the UTA DMUs had this feature many years before!). The last '108' vehicle was condemned in 1992.

Top left: *When Derby Works had to produce more 'lightweight' DMUs the result was the so-called 'new-alloy' units that later became Class 108. Two two-car sets arrive at Ilkley on a Bradford to Skipton working (no longer possible by this route) on 1 August 1959.* Author

Below: *Two Class 108 units arrive at Bolton on 20 April 1963, showing the later type units with four-digit route indicator panel above the cab windscreens.* Author

Metro-Cammell Class 101 DMUs

With 617 vehicles built, the Class 101 group of DMUs was numerically BR's largest DMU class. The Class 101 power cars had AEC diesel engines, whereas Class 102 were the otherwise identical Leyland variety. Both class numbers were soon grouped as Class 101. Both engine types were nominally 150bhp. The standard arrangement, followed by most classes of BR's diesel mechanical multiple-units, was for the engine to drive an hydraulic coupling, then a free wheel, followed by the four-speed epicyclic gearbox which drove a shaft to the final drive on the nearest axle. The final drive incorporated the reversing dogs which could be moved from one direction gear to the opposite by means of a fork worked by an electro-pneumatic drive.

The Metro-Cammell carriage bodies had a similar curved side profile to the BR standard mark 1 coaches. The bodies were integral with the underframes, all-steel and of welded construction. Insulation was by sprayed asbestos inside the body skins. They were formed into two-, three- and four-car sets. The whole class was refurbished in BR's mid 1970s scheme.

The vehicles rode on single-bolster bogies which had short swing links and no damping. They could give a lively ride. Indeed, at 60mph on 60ft worn rails the vertical and lateral ride was at times quite violent. To improve the ride, a 'Madison modification' was carried out on some of the fleet, incorporating longer swing links and lateral damping.

Class	101 Metro-Cammell DMUs
Designed for	BR
Introduced	1956
Built by	Metropolitan-Cammell
Wheel arrgt	1A-A1 (power cars)
Layout	duo-directional with one full-width cab
Engines	2 × AEC 150bhp diesels; 2 × Leyland 150bhp diesels*
Transmissions	2 × 4-speed Wilson gearboxes; reversing final drives
Max speed	70mph
Coupling code	blue square
Seats	44–65 (power cars); 45–71 (trailers)
Heating	Smith's oil-fired warm air heaters
Underframe	57ft
Weight in wo	32 tons (power cars); 25 tons (trailers)
Number built	617 vehicles
BR numbers**	50138–296, 50303–38, 50745–51, 51174–253, 51425–70, 51495–540, 51795–808 (power cars); 56050–89, 56218–20, 56332–411, 59042–55, 59060–97, 59112–31, 59302–6, 59523–68, 59586–92 (trailers)

* Leyland-engined units were first classified 102, then included in Class 101.
** In 1983, vehicles in the 50XXX series were renumbered into the 53XXX series with the final three digits unchanged; trailers in the 56XXX series became the 54XXX series.

Used on the LMR, ER, NER and ScR, and some then transferred to the WR, the 101s were successful and long-lived. Eight power cars carried parcels for two years until 1989. The last 101 was not withdrawn until December 2003, having ended its life working PTE services around Manchester.

Left: *A three-car Class 101 Metro-Cammell DMU arrives at Cloughton on a Middlesbrough to Scarborough working on 19 October 1960. This shows the fitment of two marker lamps below the windscreens which was standard on early DMUs. This one also has a two-digit route indicator in which 'B' represents a stopping passenger train.* Author

Below: *A newly-refurbished Class 101 two-car unit leaves Leeds City for Skipton in 1976, showing off its fluorescent lighting, updated décor and off-white livery.* Author

One of the characteristics of railways is that standard designs of train tend to mutate into non-standard varieties when special circumstances are confronted. In the case of the Metro-Cammell DMUs, the need to work on lines crossing the Pennine hills between Yorkshire and Lancashire led BR to agree to fit more powerful engines in a group of cars for that area. Mainly based at Bradford, 51 DMU cars were delivered in which the power cars had pairs of six-cylinder horizontal Rolls-Royce 180bhp diesel engines under the floor. These became Class 111, though, in most other respects, they were virtually identical to the 101s. Some were power-twins and others were formed power car plus trailer. Six trailer buffet cars were included in three-car sets for the North Eastern Region. In later years these were sometimes marshalled within Class 101 units. One of these buffets, No 59575, is the only preserved member of the '111' class, though of course there are several '101s' in preservation.

The last batches received four-digit route indicators above the centre cab windscreens, whereas previous end cars had relied on marker lamps and two-digit indicators below windscreen level (later removed), apart from destination blinds on the cab fronts. In common with all DMUs that survived into the late 1980s, a modification for some of these vehicles was to fit a headlamp near the centre of the lower cab front, the two-digit indicators being plated over or fully removed.

To save money, West Yorkshire Passenger Transport Executive arranged for BR to remove one engine and transmission from each of 36 of the remaining power cars and to redistribute the centre trailers

Class	111 Metro-Cammell DMUs
Designed for	BR
Introduced	1957
Built by	Metropolitan-Cammell
Wheel arrgt	1A-A1 (power cars)*
Layout	duo-directional with one full-width cab
Engines	2 × Rolls-Royce C6NFLH 180bhp diesels*
Transmissions	2 × 4-speed gearboxes; reversing final drives*
Max speed	70mph
Coupling code	blue square
Seats	52, 65 (power cars); 53,** 65 (trailers)
Heating	Smith's oil-fired warm air heaters
Underframe	57ft
Weight in wo	33 tons (power cars); 25 tons (trailers)
Number built	51 vehicles
BR numbers***	50134–37, 50270–89, 51541–60 (power cars); 56090–3, 59100–109,**** 59569–72, 59573–8** (trailers)/78706–24, 78956–74*

* From 1982, all surviving power cars were rebuilt with just one engine and transmission, becoming 2-A1 wheel arrangement.

** There were six intermediate trailers with miniature buffets.

*** In 1983, vehicles in the 50XXX series were renumbered into the 53XXX series with the final three digits unchanged; trailers in the 56XXX series became the 54XXX series.

**** Surviving trailers 59101 and 59105 in 1990 were renumbered 59110 and 59111 to avoid clashing with new Class 59/1 locomotives.

NB: In later years some trailers were marshalled in Class 101 units.

elsewhere. The lower-powered units worked as power-twins in the Leeds MetroTrain area. They were renumbered in the 78XXX series. All Class 111s had gone by 1989.

Left: *A Class 111 unit with Rolls-Royce engines arrives at Manchester London Road from Buxton on 22 April 1957. Externally these units were virtually identical to Class 101.* Author

Below: *Later Class 111s had four-digit route indicators above the cab windscreens as on this unit heading onto the Sheffield line at Doncaster in summer 1976.* Author

Class	104 BRCW DMUs
Designed for	BR
Introduced	1957
Built by	Birmingham Railway Carriage & Wagon Company
Wheel arrgt	1A-A1 (power cars)
Layout	duo-directional with one full-width cab
Engines	2 × Leyland 150bhp diesels
Transmissions	2 × 4-speed Wilson gearboxes; reversing final drives
Max speed	70mph
Coupling code	blue square
Seats	52–66 (power cars); 51–69 (trailers)
Heating	Smith's oil-fired warm air heaters
Underframe	57ft
Weight in wo	31 tons (power cars); 24, 25 tons (trailers)
Number built	302 vehicles
BR numbers*	50420–598 (power cars); 56175–189, 59132–234, 59240–244 (trailers)

* In 1983, vehicles in the 50XXX series were renumbered into the 53XXX series with the final three digits unchanged; trailers in the 56XXX series became the 54XXX series.

To speed up deliveries of DMUs as a result of the government's wish for early elimination of steam traction, all UK carriage manufacturers were given the opportunity of building DMUs for BR. The Birmingham Railway Carriage & Wagon Company (BRCW) built 302 cars to an integral steel body design that was both robust and of relatively modest weight. Known from 1968 as Class 104, the power cars had Leyland 680-type 150bhp engines, two per car, driving through the established, standard mechanical transmission.

Unusually for contemporary DMUs, the '104s' had saloon walls and partitions lined with timber veneer, making them appear darker but a bit up-market compared with other makers' DMUs.

The '104s' were normally in three- or four-car sets and worked mainly in the north of England on the London Midland and North Eastern Regions. The four-car sets in North Yorkshire were perhaps a little underpowered, particularly when hauling tail loads as was a regular practice on the Doncaster–Hull line. In the 1970s, as a result of analysis of passenger carryings, the then Eastern Region four-car sets were reduced to three cars, notably improving performance and timekeeping.

The LM Region sets worked out of Buxton and Newton Heath depots, the latter including a group that were refurbished and reliveried for Manchester–Blackpool business trains. The BRCW units were among the more reliable and steady-riding DMUs on BR, the last few surviving into the 1980s, including some that were transferred to support the Ayrshire DMU fleet in Scotland.

Top left: A three-car BRCW DMU arrives at Crewe on a service from the Chester line on 8 July 1962. This was one of the sets painted in BR's lighter green that was close to the green used on Southern Region coaching stock. Author

Left: In later years the '104s' spread far and wide due to their relative reliability. This one is passing Eldersley on a Largs to Glasgow Central working on 26 May 1984. Author

Below: This BUT Leyland diesel engine is of type 680 which represents the swept volume of its six cylinders in cubic centimetres. Many DMUs used this type of engine including the Class 104s. Ian Allan library

A BRCW Class 110 three-car unit with its four-digit route indicator showing very little useful information calls at Doncaster on a Hull to Sheffield service in 1976. These indicators were later blanked off. Author

A variation of the Class 104 design was ordered for the steeply-graded line between Leeds and Manchester through the Pennines via the Calder Valley. To cope with the gradients, the power cars had 180bhp Rolls-Royce engines driving through SE4 epicyclic gearboxes. This gave them the high power-weight ratio of 8.3bhp/ton, well suited for the hill-climbing and acceleration needed from frequent station stops.

Introduced in 1961, 20 three-car sets were allocated to the North Eastern Region and 10 to the London Midland, working out of Neville Hill and Newton Heath depots respectively. Externally they differed from the '104s' by virtue of their cab-front four-digit route indicators and by having fully-framed side windows which were a help in reducing the bodyside corrosion that affected earlier BR steel-clad carriage types. When refurbished and repainted in BR's standard blue-and-grey livery they looked very smart.

West Yorkshire Passenger Transport Executive made some savings in the early 1980s by reducing 18 of these sets to just two cars, power-twins. Later, four power cars were converted for use as parcels cars. All

Class	110 BRCW DMUs
Designed for	BR
Introduced	1961
Built by	Birmingham Railway Carriage & Wagon Company
Wheel arrgt	1A-A1 (power cars)
Layout	duo-directional with one full-width cab
Engines	2 × Rolls-Royce 180bhp diesels
Transmissions	2 × 4-speed Self-Changing Gears SE4 gearboxes; reversing final drives
Max speed	70mph
Coupling code	blue square
Seats	45–66 (power cars); 72 (trailers)
Heating	Smith's oil-fired warm air heaters
Underframe	57ft
Weight in wo	32 tons (power cars); 24 tons (trailers)
Number built	90 vehicles
BR numbers	51809–48, 52066–85 (power cars); 59693–712, 59808–817 (trailers).

the class were withdrawn around the end of the 1980s. A full three-car set is preserved on the Wensleydale Railway, and a power-twin on the Lakeside & Haverthwaite Railway.

Cravens Class 105 DMUs

Cravens of Sheffield were already producing mark 1 locomotive-hauled carriages for BR, so it was an obvious choice for one of the sources of DMUs in BR's rush to dieselise secondary line services. The mark 1 background explains Cravens' adoption of the standard BR mark 1 curved body profile. But there the similarity with the mark 1 stock ends. The Cravens DMUs had an integral body design in which the sides, roof, floor and underframe were constructed as one steel shell, several key structural members being of corrosion-resistant corten steel. The deep side windows gave the interiors plenty of light. The seating was similar to other designs of DMU, being tubular-framed seats with foam rubber cushions and backs covered in hard-wearing moquette.

Fourteen power cars had standard Leyland engines whereas the rest had AECs, both groups being of 150bhp. As with most other BR DMUs, the brake system was the Gresham & Craven quick-acting two-pipe vacuum brake. The key advantage of this design was its ability to release the brakes quickly through the train by using the vehicles' own vacuum reservoirs to exhaust the train pipe in each car, rather than waiting for an exhauster at the front of the train to drag the air out as was the practice on locomotive-hauled vacuum-braked trains.

There were 302 cars in the fleet, formed as two-car power-trailer sets and as three-car units. They worked mainly on the Eastern and LM

Class	105 Cravens DMUs
Designed for	BR
Introduced	1956
Built by	Cravens Ltd
Wheel arrgt	1A-A1 (power cars)
Layout	duo-directional with one full-width cab
Engines	2 × AEC 150bhp diesels; 2 × Leyland 150bhp diesels*
Transmissions	2 × 4-speed Wilson gearboxes; reversing final drives
Max speed	70mph
Coupling code	blue square
Seats	52, 63 (power cars); 63, 69 (trailers)
Heating	Smith's oil-fired warm air heaters
Underframe	57ft
Weight in wo	30 tons (power cars); 23, 24 tons (trailers)
Number built	302 vehicles
BR numbers**	50249, 50359–94, 50752–817, 51254–301, 51471–94 (power cars); 56114–199, 56412–483, 59307–25 (trailers)

* Leyland-engined units were first classified 106, then included in Class 105.

** In 1983, vehicles in the 50XXX series were renumbered into the 53XXX series with the final three digits unchanged; trailers in the 56XXX series became the 54XXX series.

Regions. This class was not subject to the BR refurbishing scheme in the 1970s, and all had been withdrawn by 1988. Twelve served for a time as departmental vehicles, particularly on route-learning, and nine worked as parcels units. There is a preserved Cravens twin on the East Lancashire Railway, and one driving trailer on the Llangollen Railway.

Left: *This view inside a Cravens third/standard class section shows the excellent view ahead for passengers on BR's first-generation DMUs.* Cravens/Ian Allan library

Below: *A Cravens power-trailer twin unit poses for its official photograph when new in September 1956. The nearest vehicle is No E50359. Note the speedometer drive cable from the nearest axlebox, and the bogie's angled short swing links which helped to give the '105s' their somewhat lively lateral ride.* Ian Allan library

Two batches of diesel power-twin sets were built with a single Rolls-Royce 238bhp engines under each car. The vehicles were basically the same as the 105 series, except for their power train. The first 25 two-car sets (later given the classification 112) drove through standard mechanical four-speed gearboxes, whereas the second 25 two-car units (Class 113) had hydraulic transmissions. The latter batch had a different frontal aspect because the cab front design had a large four-digit route indicator above the driver's windscreen.

These units were initially built for hilly routes in Lancashire, including services between Manchester, Accrington and Colne, and Skipton–Colne–Preston–Blackpool. Some of these were allocated to the specially converted former steam depot at Accrington. In 1967, Class 112 and 113 units were transferred to Cricklewood depot to work on north London suburban services via the London Underground 'widened lines' via St Pancras and King's Cross which were banned to the longer vehicles. Nine '112s' worked the Kentish Town–Barking line. Other units worked from Hull Botanic Gardens depot covering routes as far afield as Hornsea, York, Leeds and Doncaster.

If these units had an Achilles' heel, it was the positioning of the main drive shaft through a tunnel formed within the area occupied by the fuel tank. On occasions when the cardan shaft became disconnected

Class	112 and 113 Cravens DMUs
Designed for	BR
Introduced	1960
Built by	Cravens Ltd
Wheel arrgt	2-A1
Layout	duo-directional with one full-width cab
Engine	1 × Rolls-Royce 238bhp diesel
Transmission	1 × 4-speed gearbox (Class 112), 1 × Rolls-Royce Twin-Disc torque converter up to 46mph with direct drive above (Class 113); reversing final drive;
Max speed	70mph
Coupling code	blue square
Seats	52, 63
Heating	Smith's oil-fired warm air heaters
Underframe	57ft
Weight in wo	30 tons
Number built	100 vehicles
BR numbers	51681–730 (Class 112), 51731–780 (Class 113)

in traffic, the flaying shaft damaged the fuel tank and a number of catastrophic vehicle fires resulted. BR decided to cut its losses, and hurriedly scrapped this group of railcars in 1968 and 1969.

Above: *Approaching Potters Bar on a southbound inner suburban working to London King's Cross are two Cravens/Rolls-Royce twin sets on 15 April 1960. Later to be classified '112', these units had one 238bhp diesel under each car.* Author

Left: *A Cravens Class 113 diesel-hydraulic unit stands stabled at Kentish Town. The large four-digit route indicator carries the code for its last empty stock working and also embraces the destination blind.* J. Mitchell/Colour-Rail

Gloucester Class 100 DMUs

The Gloucester Carriage & Wagon Company delivered two batches each of 20 two-car power-trailer DMUs in 1958 and 1959. These had bodies built to an integral, all-welded steel design with no separate underframe, a practice aimed at saving weight and maximising performance. The power cars each had two AEC 150bhp diesel engines driving through standard mechanical transmissions.

The vehicles rode on typical single-bolster two-axle bogies of the same basic type as other BR 'first-generation' DMUs, though each manufacturer incorporated details that were not necessarily interchangeable with other firms' designs. Thus the ride obtained at speed varied according to how well the bogie designers had set the main bogie parameters. The Gloucester integral cars were among the better-riding units.

Most of the Class 100 units were deployed in Scotland, working from Leith depot on the Edinburgh suburban services, including to border towns such as Peebles and to Galashiels on the Waverley line. Four units worked in the Glasgow area, being allocated to Hamilton depot. One set worked the Ballater branch when the battery train was out of action. A few Gloucester sets went to the LM Region for services around the West Midlands and Manchester. The Scottish units gravitated south to Norwich and Cambridge in the late 1960s.

No Gloucester low-density units were refurbished, and most were withdrawn around 1982, the last going in 1988. Eight vehicles served in the departmental fleet in the 1980s. Two power cars and four driving trailers are held in preservation. These are made up as one two-car set each on the West Somerset Railway and at the Midland Railway Centre, and two trailers in private hands.

Class	100 Gloucester DMUs
Designed for	BR
Introduced	1956
Built by	Cravens Ltd
Wheel arrgt	1A-A1 (power cars)
Layout	duo-directional with one full-width cab
Engines	2 × AEC 150bhp diesels; 2 × Leyland 150bhp diesels*
Transmissions	2 × 4-speed Wilson gearboxes; reversing final drives
Max speed	70mph
Coupling code	blue square
Seats	52, 63 (power cars); 63, 69 (trailers)
Heating	Smith's oil-fired warm air heaters
Underframe	57ft
Weight in wo	30 tons (power cars); 23, 24 tons (trailers)
Number built	302 vehicles
BR numbers**	50249, 50359–94, 50752–817, 51254–301, 51471–94 (power cars); 56114–199, 56412–483, 59307–25 (trailers)

*   Leyland-engined units were first classified 106, then included in Class 105.

** In 1983, vehicles in the 50XXX series were renumbered into the 53XXX series with the final three digits unchanged; trailers in the 56XXX series became the 54XXX series.

Left: *The Gloucester-built two-car DMUs had steel bodies with bow-ended rooflines. The bodyside profile is flat above the waist with a sharp tumblehome at the base. In BR rail-blue livery at Crewe stands a Class 100 set on 20 July 1983 with the two-digit route-indicator blinds replaced by illuminable white disc displays.* Author

Below: *This Gloucester unit seen at Sheffield on 12 June 1989 was by then in departmental service as a saloon at the bidding of managers from the Eastern Region headquarters at York.* Author

Twenty two-car power-trailer DMUs were delivered by Park Royal from 1957. They were to an integral steel body design, with AEC 150bhp engines and standard mechanical transmission. As with most BR low-density DMUs, the vehicle interiors were lined with formica-type plastics to brighten their appearance when compared with the stained timber interiors of the locomotive-hauled carriages of the period. Also, the deep side windows giving clear views of passing scenery were popular with travellers.

A feature of all the low-density DMU classes was the arrangement of seating in the driving end areas where passengers had an almost unrestricted view through the glass partition into the full-width driving cab, and thus of the railway ahead. This proved to be very popular, giving passengers a better understanding of the railway on which they travelled. Some drivers did not like being so much in the public eye, and would pull down blinds behind them to block the view, to the chagrin of public and management alike.

Initially, the Park Royals worked from Chester depot, but four were transferred to the Cardiff and Reading areas of the Western Region.

Class	103 Park Royal DMUs
Designed for	BR
Introduced	1957
Built by	Park Royal Vehicles Limited
Wheel arrgt	1A-A1 (power cars)
Layout	duo-directional with one full-width cab
Engines	2 × AEC 150bhp diesels
Transmissions	2 × 4-speed Wilson gearboxes; reversing final drives
Max speed	70mph
Coupling code	blue square
Seats	52 (power cars); 64 (trailers)
Heating	Smith's oil-fired warm air heaters
Underframe	57ft
Weight in wo	33 tons 8cwt (power cars); 26 tons 7cwt (trailers)
Number built	40 vehicles
BR numbers	50395–414 (power cars); 56150–69 (trailers)

Others later worked the Watford–St Albans and Belmont branches after withdrawal of the ACV four-wheeled railcar sets (see page 117).

The 20 two-car Park Royal sets suffered more from body corrosion than other classes. This caused some early withdrawals beginning in the early 1970s and completed by 1983. Five vehicles were allocated to departmental work but few actually did much. Six were preserved, but of these three were later scrapped, presumably as a result of body deterioration. A twin-set rests on the Helston Railway, and one driving trailer is on the Denbigh & Mold Railway.

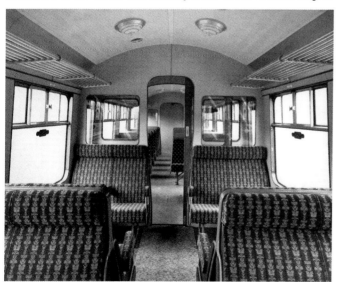

Above: *The Park Royal DMUs had integral bodies built with a side profile that was flat across the windows and gently curved below. This view shows M50395 with two broken windows as a result of vandalism in the West Midlands.* Ian Allan library

Left: *The interior of a Class 103 composite coach looking through the first class towards the standard class shows the different standards of seating.* Ian Allan library

Wickham Class 109 DMUs

A firm that made its name building small inspection and track maintenance rail vehicles was a surprise contributor to BR's DMU fleet. D. Wickham & Co of Ware in Hertfordshire built five two-car power-trailer DMUs of unusual body design in that the construction was totally integral, the body, roof and floor design being able to take all buffing, traction and bending stresses without needing a separate underframe. This enabled the weight to be held low, the power cars being no more than 27½ tons weight and the driving trailers just 20½ tons. These trains had a tubular steel body framework that was designed to resist corrosion, and were fitted with fully-framed side windows and windscreens from the start. All five went to the Eastern Region. Their duties included a spell on the Upminster to Romford line.

Each power car had two Leyland 150bhp horizontal diesel engines under the floor, each engine driving through an hydraulic coupling (fluid flywheel) and the normal Wilson four-speed epicyclic gearbox with a free wheel and a reversing final drive on each driven axle. The bogies were single-bolster bogies of similar design to other DMUs except that the designers added vertical hydraulic dampers connecting the swing bolster with the bogie frame. These were to control both bounce and sway, and proved their worth because this group of railcars rode noticeably better than the rest.

Two of these units were later sold to the railways of Trinidad who had an urgent need for lightweight railcars. The remaining three units proved

Class	109 Wickham DMUs
Designed for	BR
Introduced	1957
Built by	D. Wickham & Company
Wheel arrgt	1A-A1 (power cars)
Layout	duo-directional with one full-width cab
Engines	2 × Leyland 150bhp diesels
Transmissions	2 × 4-speed Wilson gearboxes; reversing final drives
Max speed	70mph
Coupling code	blue square
Seats	59 (power cars); 66 (trailers)
Heating	Smith's oil-fired warm air heaters
Underframe	57ft
Weight in wo	27 tons 10cwt (power cars); 20 tons 10cwt (trailers)
Number built	10 vehicles
BR numbers*	50415–19 (power cars); 56170–74 (trailers).

* E50416+E56171 became a departmental saloon from 1966 to 1980, numbered DB975005–6.

costly to repair when subjected to collision damage and were withdrawn in 1970 as non-standard. One unit became part of departmental stock and was converted to form a luxury inspection unit, for a while based at Doncaster as the divisional manager's saloon. This unique unit has been preserved and restored close to its original condition. It is in service on the Llangollen Railway.

Left: Among the lightest DMUs built for BR's modernisation plan were the five two-car units from Wickham's of Ware. They were also the best riding by dint of intelligent placement of hydraulic dampers. Driving trailer No E56171 brings up the rear of the shuttle service from Romford after arrival at Upminster on 8 March 1958. The oil tail-lamp set on its bracket appears to be partially obscured by the large buffer head! Author

Below: The Eastern Region Doncaster divisional manager's saloon for several years was the last surviving Wickham DMU, numbered DB975005–6. The interior had been upgraded to enable official guests to be suitably accommodated. J. W. Millbank/Colour-Rail

British Railways engineers soon realised that a three-car DMU with two twin-engined power cars and an intermediate trailer vehicle would have a high enough power/weight ratio to perform reasonably well without expensive engineering solutions to reduce the vehicle weights. Derby Carriage Works produced the first batch of 42 suburban DMUs in 1957, followed quickly by further batches until there were 104 three-car sets in service. This design was specifically for suburban work in areas with no electric network such as Birmingham, Glasgow and west London. By building longer underframes, 64ft in length, and fitting steel bodies with slam doors to each seating bay, and using the by-then normal seating arrangement of 3+2 across the vehicles, high carrying capacity was available at a reasonable price. Thus was born the design that became the Class 116. For further builds by other manufacturers, BR specified the design in more detail than it had done in the urgent days of ordering the low-density units. Thus the companies of Gloucester, BRCW and Pressed Steel, which also entered the DMU construction phase at this time in 1959, all built suburban DMUs to basically the same design. All had 150bhp Leyland engines and standard mechanical transmission.

However, when it came to needing four-car suburban units for services out of Marylebone and St Pancras stations in north London, two 150bhp engines under each of the outer cars were simply not enough to secure acceptable acceleration from station stops. For these units, different solutions were adopted.

In 1959 a batch of four-car sets was introduced for the St Pancras–Bedford route. To gain the extra power needed, each of the two power cars in each set had two Rolls-Royce 238bhp diesel engines driving through Twin-Disc torque converter transmissions. On the other hand, the Marylebone sets, also built by Derby Works, had two Leyland Albion 230bhp engines driving through four-speed mechanical gearboxes.

The suburban DMUs with the highest power/weight ratio were the Lea Valley sets, a batch of three-car sets with the same Rolls-Royce engines as the 'Bed-Pan' sets. The Lea Valley units worked until 1977 on the Liverpool Street–Cheshunt and Epping routes, together with the Southminster services.

Withdrawal of the main groups of high-density DMUs came when more modern DMUs were introduced by BR, mainly of the Class 150 series (see Chapter 11), or when local areas were electrified. Electrification certainly caused the withdrawal of the St Pancras and Liverpool Street DMUs, but the Marylebone sets lasted until displaced by Class 165s.

One might argue that in the late 1950s and early 1960s the concept of having lots of slam doors along suburban trains was already outmoded. Bear in mind the UTA MED trains (page 28) which had sliding doors from 1952, as indeed did LMS EMUs working the Wirral lines from 1938, let alone the London Underground trains. But BR seemed wedded to slam doors, possibly because of the Southern Region's insistence that boarding and alighting times were quicker with these. The longer dwell times with which we are familiar in the 21st century would appear to support the SR's view, but for passenger safety surely sliding doors are much superior.

High-density DMUs were the norm on routes where high capacity was needed for relatively short journeys. This Derby-built Class 115 four-car set is working from London Marylebone to Princes Risborough, passing Saunderton in July 1964. This demonstrates the four-digit indicator in full use. G. S. Cocks/Colour-Rail

Derby Class 116 DMUs

BR's first suburban DMUs were what would later be known as the Class 116. These were all three-car sets. Built at Derby, the '116s' had steel girder underframes riding on standard single-bolster DMU bogies. The conventional steel-framed steel-clad bodies had single slam doors to each seating bay. The cars were initially non-gangwayed on the grounds that for suburban work train crews and passengers did not need to move through the train. In later years this idea fell by the wayside; the introduction of on-train ticket sales (remember 'pay trains'?) led to gangways being fitted, the last being a group of LM Region sets based at Tyseley in 1983. By this time several sets had received intermediate trailers from redundant Class 127 DMUs following the St Pancras–Bedford electrification.

The body profile followed a more conventional shape, similar to the LMS Stanier carriage profile, flat along the side windows area though leaning towards the centre to keep the cantrail inside the loading gauge, and with a pronounced tumblehome at the bottom of the bodysides. The bodies were on 64ft-long underframes and most seats were arranged 3+2 across the centre aisle with seats facing each other in each bay. The cab front featured windscreens that leaned back at a small angle from the vertical.

The first sets had four marker lamps, one centrally above the centre cab windscreen and three evenly spaced along the lower cab front. Later batches had two-digit route code boxes below the centre windscreen, and only the two outer bottom marker lamps. These latter became electric tail lamps about the time that headlamps were fitted. Until then, oil tail lamps were placed on lamp irons at the rear of each train.

Class	116 Derby DMUs
Designed for	BR
Introduced	1957
Built by	BR Derby
Wheel arrgt	1A-A1 (power cars)
Layout	duo-directional with one full-width cab
Engines	2 × Leyland 150bhp diesels
Transmissions	2 × 4-speed Wilson gearboxes; reversing final drives
Max speed	70mph
Coupling code	blue square
Seats	65, 89, 95 (power cars); 98, 102 (trailers)
Heating	Smith's oil-fired warm air heaters
Underframe	64ft
Weight in wo	36 tons 0cwt (power cars); 28 tons 10cwt (trailers)
Number built	320 vehicles
BR numbers*	50050–133, 50870–923, 51128–53 (power cars); 59000–41, 59326–76, 59438–48 (trailers)

* In 1983, vehicles in the 50XXX series were renumbered into the 53XXX series with the final three digits unchanged.

While at first allocated for services around Birmingham and in South Wales, the '116s' ended up on all Regions except the Southern. The last was withdrawn during the 1990s. Seven power cars and four trailers are preserved.

Left: *Among the earliest Derby long-underframe suburban DMUs was a batch of three-car sets for the Western Region area based at Birmingham Snow Hill. One is seen arriving there on 30 August 1955. This type later became Class 116.* Author

Below: *A Class 116 Derby-built high-density DMU repainted in BR blue-and-grey approaches Paisley on a service to Ardrossan Harbour in October 1980.* Author

Class	117 Pressed Steel DMUs
Designed for	BR
Introduced	1959
Built by	Pressed Steel
Wheel arrgt	1A-A1 (power cars)
Layout	duo-directional with one full-width cab
Engines	2 × Leyland 150bhp diesels
Transmissions	2 × 4-speed Wilson gearboxes; reversing final drives
Max speed	70mph
Coupling code	blue square
Seats	65, 89, 91 (power cars); 70, 74 (trailers)
Heating	Smith's oil-fired warm air heaters
Underframe	64ft
Weight in wo	36 tons (power cars); 30 tons (trailers)
Number built	123 vehicles
BR numbers	51332–415 (power cars); 59484–522 (trailers)*

* The three power-twin sets were made up to three-car units by insertion of Class 118 trailers 59478/9/80. Also, former GWR corridor coaches Nos W7254W, W7804W and W7813W were observed to be in use as Class 117 intermediate trailer cars in 1961, making up three four-car sets. These GWR vehicles had previously worked in Class 119 Cross-Country sets.

Built to a very similar design to the '116s', the 42 sets that would later become Class 117 were ordered from the Pressed Steel Company of Linwood in Scotland. Visually they were the same as the '116s' except that they had either no lamps or two lamps on the cab fronts. They also had four-digit train number displays situated above the cab front windscreens. Three of the sets worked for a time with former GWR carriages as intermediate trailer cars.

The '117s' worked for a long time on Paddington suburban services, being based at Southall depot. The class was later rebuilt with gangways between cars. They were extremely long-lived, in their last few years venturing as far afield as the Edinburgh suburban network. Many survived to as late as 1999, but were put into storage at the start of the 21st century.

As a result of their long lives, the '117s' bore more liveries than most DMUs in their lifetime. Beginning with BR lined dark green, they succumbed to the all-over rail blue era before receiving the more attractive blue-and-grey colours. Later those working on the WR were decked in Network SouthEast red-white-and-blue. Those that went to the Fife services received Regional Railways livery. One three-car set based at Tyseley was repainted in GWR brown-and-cream to mark the GW150 event.

Three power cars were taken into departmental stock to work as water-jetting vehicles on the Chiltern lines.

Because of their long working lives, more than half of the '117s' benefited from being extant in the peak of the preservation era. Thirty-three power cars are preserved, together with 25 intermediate trailer cars, representing the most numerous class of preserved first-generation BR DMUs.

Above left: *A surprise for railway enthusiasts at Bournemouth on 24 June 1967 was when a Western Region Class 117 DMU worked an excursion from the London area, seen leaving the resort's Central station.* Alan Thorpe

Below: *Equally surprising was the repaint given to Tyseley-based 117 305, seen bearing GWR colours at Birmingham New Street in 1993. This class was built by the Pressed Steel Company of Linwood, Scotland.* Author

At Pembroke Dock on 26 October 1984 stands BRCW Class 118 three-car unit No B472. Allocated to Bristol St Philip's Marsh depot, this unit was on a diagram that took it a long way through South Wales. *Author*

Class	118 BRCW DMUs
Designed for	BR
Introduced	1960
Built by	Birmingham Railway Carriage & Wagon Company
Wheel arrgt	1A-A1 (power cars)
Layout	duo-directional with one full-width cab
Engines	2 × Leyland 150bhp diesels
Transmissions	2 × 4-speed Wilson gearboxes; reversing final drives
Max speed	70mph
Coupling code	blue square
Seats	65, 89 (power cars); 70 (trailers)
Heating	Smith's oil-fired warm air heaters
Underframe	64ft
Weight in wo	36 tons (power cars); 30 tons (trailers)
Number built	45 vehicles
BR numbers	51302–51331 (power cars); 59469–83 (trailers)

NB: Three Class 118 trailers, Nos 59478–80, normally ran in Class 117 units.

Fifteen three-car sets of similar design to the Classes 116 and 117 were built by the Birmingham Railway Carriage & Wagon Company in 1960. They differed only slightly from the '117s' in that BRCW decorated their interiors with laminated wood, in similar fashion to the same manufacturer's Class 104s. Other low- and high-density DMUs generally had plastic laminate interior panelling, thought at the time to be harder wearing and visually lighter and more modern.

Like the '117s', the '118s' had four-digit train describer boxes at the top of the cab fronts. Each power car had two marker lamps, one above either buffer, though some only received these a few years into their service. The standard formation was as other suburban three-car sets, a driving motor brake second (DMBS), driving motor second (DMS) and trailer composite (TC) which, as well as the usual 3+2 second-class seating, had a saloon with 12 first-class seats in 2+2 layout.

The '118s' were split between Plymouth Laira, Bristol St Philip's Marsh and Reading depots. Three Class 118 intermediate trailer cars were transferred to make up three-car Class 117 units. The resultant two-car power-twin '118s' saw service on lower-trafficked West Country branch lines.

These were quite long-lasting vehicles, many serving into the mid-1990s, the last being withdrawn in 1994. Two power cars became departmental vehicles (51306 renumbered 977752 and 51321 renumbered 977753); these were fitted for dispensing Sandite friction paste to the rail heads to improve wheel/rail adhesion during the autumn, a time of year when, due to heavy leaf fall, rail head conditions are at their worst.

Driving motor second No 51331 was subsequently preserved and at the time of writing (June 2010) resides on the Battlefield Railway.

With bodies, underframes and bogies virtually the same as Class 116, the 20 'Lea Valley' DMUs had more powerful diesel engines and hydraulic transmissions, being intended to work on routes already served by electric trains and with the steeply graded climb through Bethnal Green. Under each power car were two Rolls-Royce 238bhp diesel engines driving through two Rolls-Royce Twin-Disc torque converters. They were designated for the routes out of London's Liverpool Street station to Hertfordshire through the Lea Valley. Destinations included Cheshunt, Epping, Hertford East, Bishop's Stortford and Southminster.

The trains carried a dull livery of plain BR dark green with 'whiskers' on the cab front; cab roofs were initially painted white. The cab-front decoration was soon replaced with small yellow warning panels. Early on in the rail-blue era from 1966, in common with all BR trains at the time, full yellow cab fronts were applied. Unlike the '116' to '118' class groups, these non-gangwayed sets remained thus, no unit being converted with gangways.

Then came the Great Eastern electrification scheme, which displaced these DMUs near the end of the 1960s. Work was found for them on the suburban lines out of King's Cross. When the former GNR main and suburban lines were electrified, the Class 125s were withdrawn between late 1976 and early 1977.

Two trailer cars, 59448/66, were taken into departmental stock and used for testing fire resistant materials. No Class 125 is preserved.

Class	125 Derby DMUs
Designed for	BR
Introduced	1958
Built by	BR Derby
Wheel arrgt	1A-A1 (power cars)
Layout	duo-directional with one full-width cab
Engines	2 × Rolls-Royce 238bhp diesels
Transmissions	2 × Rolls-Royce Twin-Disc torque converters; reversing final drives
Max speed	70mph
Coupling code	orange star
Seats	65, 95 (power cars); 106 (trailers)
Heating	Smith's oil-fired warm air heaters
Underframe	64ft
Weight in wo	35 tons 10cwt (power cars); 28 tons 10cwt (trailers)
Number built	60 vehicles
BR numbers	50988–51007, 51154–73 (power cars); 59449–68 (trailers).

The Derby-built Class 125 DMUs had more powerful engines, originally to handle the acceleration needed to keep them ahead of electric trains on the Great Eastern Division. Later on the Great Northern main line, this pair of units heads for Royston through Wood Green station on 19 September 1969. David Percival

Gloucester Class 122 and Pressed Steel Class 121 railcars

In 1958, 20 single-vehicle two-cab diesel railcars were delivered by Gloucester Railway Carriage & Wagon Company. These were basically similar to the BR Class 116 suburban cars except for their two cabs and AEC diesel engines. A batch of nine driving trailer vehicles also appeared for use with the single power cars at times of heavier traffic. BR ordered 15 more from Pressed Steel which emerged in 1960, together with 10 more driving trailers. The Pressed Steel cars later became Class 121, and the Gloucester vehicles Class 122, the respective driving trailers being Classes 149 and 150 though use of these two class numbers quickly fell by the wayside.

The first units went to Western Region branches in the London area. Later the vehicles spread all round the country as they were displaced from branches that were affected by the 1960s railway closures. They also worked occasionally in suburban three-car DMU sets when other power cars were out of action. Despite the low capacity of single or two-car rail vehicles, some of these DMUs survived into the 1990s on such workings as Bletchley–Bedford, Stockport–Stalybridge, and the Cornish branches. Indeed, six of them were used for a few seasons to replace 'Pacer' two-axle DMUs when the latter caused problems on sharply-curved lines in Cornwall.

Withdrawals were steady during the 1970s and 1980s, the last three being condemned after departmental working in 1993. However, two have since been reinstated to active passenger service. Refurbished Class 121 No 55020 is with Chiltern Railways working between Princes Risborough and Aylesbury. Arriva Trains Wales is using No 55032 on its shuttle service between Cardiff Queen Street and Cardiff Bay stations.

Class	122 and 121* single DMUs
Designed for	BR
Introduced	1958, 1960*
Built by	Gloucester Railway Carriage & Wagon Co, Pressed Steel Co*
Wheel arrgt	1A-A1 (power cars)
Layout	duo-directional with two full-width cabs**
Engines	2 × AEC 150bhp diesels***
Transmissions	2 × 4-speed Wilson gearboxes; reversing final drives
Max speed	70mph
Coupling code	blue square
Seats	65 (power cars); 95 then 91; 93, then 89 (trailers)*
Heating	Smith's oil-fired warm air heaters
Underframe	64ft
Weight in wo	37 tons 8cwt; 36 tons* (power cars); 29 tons 7cwt; 29 tons* (trailers)
Number built	20 × 122; 9 driving trailers; 15 × 121; 10 driving trailers
BR numbers	55000–19; 55020–35* (power cars); 56291–299; 56280–89* (driving trailers).

*   Details refer to Class 121.
**   Driving trailers had one cab.
*** Some vehicles later had Leyland 150bhp diesel engines.

These are the only first-generation DMUs still in regular passenger use on the national railway network, as opposed to preservation where there are four 121s, six 122s and three Pressed Steel driving trailers still extant.

Top: The Class 121 series of single power cars came from Pressed Steel to a similar design to the '116s' but with two cabs. This view of No W55030 at Oxford on 24 September 1961 shows the way the twin exhaust pipes ran up in front of the cab windscreens at one end of the car. Author

Right: No 55010 was a single car built by the Gloucester C&W Co. It was photographed at Dundee depot on 26 August 1980 and was designated Class 122. Author

Two four-car sets of Class 127 stand at London St Pancras station on 9 July 1960 between duties on the Bedford route. The leading vehicle is M51632. These Derby-built units had Rolls-Royce engines and hydraulic transmissions with direct drive at the higher running speeds. Author

Introduced in 1959, the four-car DMUs for the London St Pancras–Bedford service were normal Derby-designed high-density vehicles but with more powerful traction to cope with the additional trailer vehicle. The power cars each had two Rolls-Royce eight-cylinder horizontal 238bhp diesel engines, driving through RR DFR10000 series torque converters. At 46mph the drive changed automatically to direct drive; the driver had to throttle back briefly to permit this to happen.

The '127s' were initially branded with the blue square coupling code because they were wired so that standard mechanical DMUs could run in multiple with them. This posed no problem when being driven from the mechanical geared unit, but some drivers did not get on well with driving a multiple train from the '127' end; it was possible as the train accelerated for the driver to forget that he had a mechanical unit in multiple at the rear, and thus on occasions when the driver forgot to throttle back and change gear at each stage, the mechanical unit could be driven at speeds faster than those for which the lower gears were intended. At least one vehicle fire was caused by this forgetfulness. Thereafter the '127s' were given the red triangle coupling code.

The units were maintained at a new depot at Cricklewood. Internally they were more modern than earlier DMUs in that they had fluorescent lighting from new instead of the familiar tungsten bulbs. The '127s' remained non-

Class	127 Derby DMUs
Designed for	BR
Introduced	1959
Built by	BR Derby
Wheel arrgt	1A-A1 (power cars)
Layout	duo-directional with one full-width cab
Engines	2 × Rolls-Royce 238bhp diesels
Transmissions	2 × Rolls-Royce Twin-Disc torque converters; reversing final drives
Max speed	70mph
Coupling code	blue square/red triangle*
Seats	76, 78 (power cars); 90, 106 (trailers)
Heating	Smith's oil-fired warm air heaters
Underframe	64ft
Weight in wo	40 tons (power cars); 28, 29 tons (trailers)
Number built	120 vehicles
BR numbers	51591–650 (power cars); 59589–648 (trailers)

* In 1969 the '127s' received the red triangle coupling code to prevent coupling to other classes of DMU following a serious fire.

gangwayed throughout their lives, though a few trailer cars that found their way into other DMU sets were modified to suit later in life.

Several cars were withdrawn piecemeal from 1966 onwards due to accidents and fires, but the main fleet withdrawal came when the Bedford–St Pancras service was electrified in 1983. Eight power cars and two trailers are preserved.

BR Class 115 DMUs

For the suburban services out of London Marylebone station, BR ordered 41 four-car DMUs sets from Derby Works which became Class 115. Six sets were also allocated to work on the former Cheshire Lines Committee route between Liverpool and Manchester. As with the '127s' (page 51), the '115s' needed more powerful engines to ensure they could perform well as four-car units and received Leyland Albion engines of 230bhp. These drove through four-speed epicyclic mechanical gearboxes in the normal way. They were blue square coupling code units and so could multiple with most DMU types.

Internally, serving as they did the up-market Chiltern dormitory towns, BR fitted passenger seating that eschewed the bus-seat image of the other high-density DMUs. These were heavy seats with solid-looking armrests, laid out four to a bay in second (later standard) class and in the normal 2+1 layout in first class. Like the '127s' they had fluorescent lighting.

The Allerton-based CLC-route units had one diagram at weekends that took them right across the country to Hull. Another, among the Marylebone-based units, was used towards the end of the Great Central main line's existence as a through route, on a London–Nottingham

Class	115 Derby DMUs
Designed for	BR
Introduced	1960
Built by	BR Derby
Wheel arrgt	1A-A1 (power cars)
Layout	duo-directional with one full-width cab
Engines	2 × Leyland Albion 230bhp diesels
Transmissions	2 × SCG four-speed gearboxes; reversing final drives
Max speed	70mph
Coupling code	blue square
Seats	78 (power cars); 70, 106 (trailers)
Heating	Smith's oil-fired warm air heaters
Underframe	64ft
Weight in wo	38 tons (power cars); 28, 29 tons (trailers)
Number built	164 vehicles
BR numbers	51651–80, 51849–900 (power cars); 59649–78, 59713–64 (trailers).

service. Both of these longer-distance journeys were surely unsuitable for DMUs with no corridor connections and toilets that were only available to a proportion of their passengers!

When displaced from the Chiltern Lines routes by new Class 165 and 166 DMUs from 1991 to 1992, some sets transferred to work Birmingham cross-city services. These survived until 1994. Ten power cars and six trailers are preserved.

A Class 115 unit for the Chiltern Lines works the 12.30pm from London Marylebone to High Wycombe between Gerrard's Cross and Seer Green on 9 November 1963. These higher-powered DMUs were successful at this work. Brian Stephenson

Until 1956, the use of diesel multiple-units on fast, quality inter-urban services had occurred in a small way only on the Great Western Railway and in Ireland. From 1954, BR had concentrated on secondary and branch lines for its DMU applications. Probably with an eye on what was being achieved in Ireland, where diesel railcar trains of up to eight vehicles were running on express services between Dublin and Cork, for example, BR set out to improve the Glasgow–Edinburgh main line with specially designed DMU trains.

Dieselisation of the popular fast route between Edinburgh and Glasgow, the direct line through Falkirk High, required the potential to provide fast trains with a good level of passenger comfort. BR's Swindon Works designed and built 64 steel vehicles specifically for this service. The power cars each had two 150bhp AEC diesels. These trains were made up into six-car sets, normally with full-width cabs on the two outer end power cars. Two intermediate power cars with gangways and half-width cabs provided a much-needed power boost and two trailers including a buffet were in the middle of each set. This formation gave a power/weight ratio of 5.47bhp/ton, somewhat on the low side for such a prestigious duty.

The Inter-City units, as these were dubbed, were on heavy underframes similar to mark 1 coaching stock, with Pullman-type gangways and buckeye couplings. Because each power car generated its own control air supply, the units were incompatible with other DMUs; thus they had the unique white-circle coupling code.

A further batch of three-car Inter-City sets started work on Birmingham–South Wales services before joining the rest of that group on the Glasgow–Ayr–Stranraer line, a hilly route that sorely taxed their engines and transmissions.

A nine-coach formation of '126s' crosses the moorland near Barrhill while working a Stranraer Harbour to Glasgow Central service on 10 April 1982. Author

In 1958 Swindon delivered some more heavyweight three-car units, this time under the Cross-Country banner. These were not gangwayed at the outer ends and had conventional screw couplings and the normal blue-square coupling code and were thus compatible with the majority of BR DMUs. They became Class 120 and worked in the Western Region, and in Scotland between Inverness and Aberdeen, and spread more widely in later years, working on the LM Region.

In parallel, the Gloucester Railway Carriage & Wagon Company built a further batch of Cross-Country units, Class 119, which saw service almost totally on the Western Region. These worked Bristol–Weymouth and Cardiff–Portsmouth services, as well as various secondary and branch lines in the West Country, the West Midlands and Wales. Later in their lives they served on the Reading to Gatwick Airport line.

All these units were comfortable to ride in, especially in the deeply-padded first-class seats. Most had the conventional DMU forward view past the driver, except for some of the early Scottish Class 126s which had brake vans located at the vehicle outer ends. Their Achilles' heel was the low power/weight ratio. Even on an inter-urban route such as Crewe–Derby, the author recalls some very laborious climbs upgrade from Stoke-on-Trent to Longton in Class 120 units when one engine was out of action, not an uncommon problem with these multi-engined units.

BR Class 126 Inter-City DMUs

When delivered, the Southern green Inter-City DMUs in Scotland caused quite a stir. They were the first quality inter-urban DMUs in the UK. They enabled the Scottish Region to set up a half-hourly interval service between Edinburgh and Glasgow. Maybe the cab front was a bit bland, with just a stencilled letter 'A' denoting its Class 1 express train status, and no other marker lamps or route indicators.

The four power cars in each set weighed 38 tons each, with two 150bhp AEC diesel engines under the floor driving through standard mechanical transmissions. At 33 tons 8cwt, the trailers were typical of main line carriages of that era, but heavier than the norm set by other low-density DMUs. They could not be coupled to any other DMU vehicle types. (An aberration was the fact that mechanically the jumpers could be coupled to those on blue square coded units, but the wires in the jumpers served different purposes and control chaos resulted when a driver did so!)

The cars had buckeye couplings and Pullman-type gangways, which would have made it easier for crews to couple and uncouple them, not something done frequently in practice while in E&G service. They became part of Class 126 and, after a period in Brunswick green, eventually ended up in rail blue-and-grey livery.

Bearing in mind that these quite heavy vehicles had bus engines for power, it was not surprising that they became increasingly unreliable. In 1971 they were replaced on the Edinburgh–Glasgow route by push-

In original condition and painted in the lighter multiple-unit green, a five-car Edinburgh–Glasgow Inter-City DMU stands at Eastfield depot on 10 July 1960. Each unit was normally formed of six cars, four power cars and two trailers including a buffet. Author

Class	126 Inter-City DMUs
Designed for	BR
Introduced	1956
Built by	BR Swindon
Wheel arrgt	1A-A1 (power cars)
Layout (end cars)	duo-directional with one full-width cab
(inner power cars)	duo-directional with one half-width cab
Engines	2 × AEC 150bhp diesels
Transmissions	2 × 4-speed Wilson gearboxes; reversing final drives
Max speed	70mph
Coupling code	white circle
Seats	52, 64 (power cars); 32 (trailer buffets), 42, 50 (other trailers)
Heating	Smith's oil-fired warm air heaters
Underframe	64ft
Weight in wo	38 tons (power cars); 34 tons (trailer buffets), 33 tons 8cwt (trailer firsts)
Number built	64 vehicles (E&G); 69 (Ayr)
BR numbers (E&G)	79083–111, 79155–68 (power cars); 79440–7 (trailer buffets), 79470–82 (trailer firsts);
BR numbers (Ayr)	50936, 51008–51 (power cars); 59098–9 (trailer buffets), 59391–412 (other trailers).

pull trains of modified mark 2 stock with a Class 27 diesel locomotive at each end. Only four survived beyond 1972, being transferred to Ayr depot to augment the later batch of '126s' there. One E&G car, No. 79443, survives in preservation under the care of the Scottish Railway Preservation Society and is based at the Bo'ness & Kinneil Railway. Five end cars went to Liberia, where some remained in derelict condition in 2010.

Top: *The Cardiff–Birmingham '126s' were formed as three-car sets with an intermediate car at one end. They were soon reallocated to Ayrshire services in Scotland. This one is leading an Ayr service leaving Glasgow Central in 1981.* Author

Middle: *The intermediate power cars had end gangways with half-width cabs, such as this one leading a service from Glasgow Central into Ayr, still carrying plain BR blue livery in 1976.* Author

Bottom: *By the 1980s the use of the end gangways on '126s' was no longer required by the operators; complaints about draughts from the gangways alongside the driving cabs inspired a modification to fit blanking plates. In 1981, this modified one arrives at Glasgow Central from Ayr.* Author

Three years after the Edinburgh–Glasgow Inter-City DMUs were delivered, Swindon Works produced a further batch, this time for the Glasgow–Ayr–Stranraer route though they worked at first between Cardiff and Birmingham. They were basically the same as the E&G sets, except that they always operated as three-car sets, often in multiples of two or three units. At the full-width cab end of each unit, the guard's brake compartment was at the rear of the carriage so that first-class passengers could see forward past the driver.

Each three-car set was made up of an end driving power car, a trailer car and an intermediate driving power car. It became difficult for the operators to multiple sets with the intermediate power cars always in the middle of the train. After a couple of decades of not reliably being able to join two sets gangway-to-gangway, the end gangways were dispensed with. The space in the cab front was covered with a blanking plate.

Two of the Ayr sets were delivered with buffet cars, presumably for the Glasgow–Stranraer boat trains, but these were soon downgraded to normal seating vehicles. The trains were delivered in green and all were subsequently repainted plain rail blue by BR. From around 1980 the whole fleet was repainted during overhauls in the standard blue-and-grey livery. None of the '126s' was refurbished, apart from the normal periodic overhauls in Glasgow Works.

The '126s' were underpowered for the hilly Stranraer road. Starting southbound out of Girvan, for example, they had to remain in second gear for several miles of the 1 in 50 climb.

With their control wiring deteriorating seriously, they were finally withdrawn by the end of 1983, being replaced by other classes of DMU drafted in from elsewhere until electrification in 1986. A full three-car unit is preserved on the Bo'ness & Kinneil Railway west of Edinburgh.

BR Class 120 Cross-Country DMUs

The author first rode on a Swindon Cross-Country DMU in 1960 from Inverness to Aberdeen. He and his friend were impressed by the gentle ride and comfort of the unit. The unit was one of the seven Scottish-allocated sets and was painted in lined Brunswick green. Later, the fleet received the brighter Southern-type green and then, in the late-1960s, BR rail blue and lastly blue-and-grey from the early 1980s.

Previously, in 1958, the Western Region had begun to receive its first batch of 49 sets. The last batch of 9 sets came in 1961. While they looked similar externally to the Class 126 Inter-City units, their body and underframe design was fundamentally different, being of integral construction and therefore slightly lighter. Whereas the '126s' had retractable side buffers and buckeye couplings, the '120s' reverted to screw couplings and hydraulic buffers.

All the Class 120s ran as three-car sets made up of two power cars and a centre trailer with small buffet, though the buffet section was later replaced by seating. The power cars each had two 150bhp AEC engines and Wilson four-speed epicyclic gearboxes. Later some of the cars were re-engined with Leyland engines of the same power output. A few sets, mainly ScR ones, were refurbished and stripped of asbestos insulation.

The WR sets worked in most directions from Birmingham and Cardiff, including some on the Central Wales line. When the Aberdeen–Inverness service went over to locomotive haulage from 1980, the ScR's sets

Class	120 Cross-Country DMUs
Designed for	BR
Introduced	1958
Built by	BR Swindon
Wheel arrgt	1A-A1 (power cars)
Layout	duo-directional with one full-width cab
Engines	2 × AEC 150bhp diesels*
Transmissions	2 × 4-speed Wilson gearboxes; reversing final drives
Max speed	70mph
Coupling code	blue square
Seats	34, 68 (power cars); 64 (trailer buffets)
Heating	Smith's oil-fired warm air heaters
Underframe	64.5ft
Weight in wo	36 tons 10cwt, 36 tons (power cars); 31 tons (trailer buffets)
Number built	194 vehicles
BR numbers	50647–744, 51573–90, 51781–94 (power cars); 59255–301, 59579–588, 59679–685.

* Later replaced by Leyland 680-type 150bhp diesel engines.

Swindon Works built 64 three-car units for Cross-Country services, seven for the Aberdeen–Inverness line and the rest for the WR, though they became more scattered later. This one awaits departure from Derby on a service to Crewe in August 1976. Author

went south, some to the LMR. Many of the WR sets went to the LMR as well, and by the mid-1980s they were to be seen over a wide area from Blackpool across to Lincoln.

A few went to Scotland in early 1986 to enable the '126s' there to be scrapped, but were themselves withdrawn following the Ayr route electrification, the last being condemned in 1989. Eight power cars spent a few years on parcels-carrying duties. Only one vehicle is preserved: buffet trailer No 59276 is on the Great Central Railway.

The Gloucester Carriage & Wagon Company won a contract to build further Cross-Country units which became Class 119. A typical working for these was the Weymouth to Bristol run on which this unit was photographed on 10 October 1959 while climbing Bruton incline after joining the WR Berks & Hants main line at Castle Cary. Author

Class	119 Cross-Country DMUs
Designed for	BR
Introduced	1958
Built by	Gloucester Carriage & Wagon Co Ltd
Wheel arrgt	1A-A1 (power cars)
Layout	duo-directional with one full-width cab
Engines	2 × AEC 150bhp diesels*
Transmissions	2 × 4-speed Wilson gearboxes; reversing final drives
Max speed	70mph
Coupling code	blue square
Seats	34, 68 (power cars); 64 (trailer buffets)
Heating	Smith's oil-fired warm air heaters
Underframe	64.5ft
Weight in wo	37 tons, 38 tons (power cars); 31 tons (trailer buffets)
Number built	81 vehicles
BR numbers	51052–107 (power cars); 59413–37.

* Later replaced by Leyland 680-type 150bhp diesel engines.

Only a few months later than the '120s', the Gloucester Carriage & Wagon Company delivered the first of its Cross-Country sets to the Western Region. These later became Class 119. Structurally they followed the basic Derby design layout for the suburban sets, except for the '119s'' wide side windows and limited number of passenger doors. Fifty-six power cars were built, enough for 28 sets, but only 25 trailer cars were provided, so some sets ran as power-twins.

Internally they appeared slightly more austere than the '120s'. The Gloucester cars did not have window curtains in standard class, only pull-down blinds (in line with contemporary locomotive-hauled stock).

The Class 119s ran most of their careers based at the Western Region. They virtually monopolised the Bristol-Weymouth service and served on many West Country branch lines. In London outer suburban service some sets worked between Paddington and Oxford. These were strengthened to four cars by the addition of a Hawksworth ex-GWR composite carriage, suitably modified, within the formation.

Having been insulated heavily with sprayed blue asbestos on the body interiors, the realisation by BR that this substance was hazardous to humans led to many of the class being prematurely withdrawn. A small group of sets,

having been stripped of asbestos and given a light refurbishment inside, were allocated to Reading depot for the Reading to Gatwick Airport service. These were the last survivors of the class, and worked on this service until displaced around 1992 by new Class 165 DMUs. By this time the remaining '119s' were decked in the red-white-and-blue livery of Network SouthEast.

Three power cars are preserved, two on the Swindon & Cricklade Railway and one at Wirksworth.

BR Class 124 Trans-Pennine DMUs

Introduced in 1960, the Trans-Pennine DMUs caused great interest because they dramatically reduced travel time, by some 20 minutes, on the route linking Hull with Leeds, Manchester and Liverpool. The 1,840 installed brake horsepower that was available on these sets made it possible for the trains to run up the Pennine hills at speeds that were only dreamed of previously. Just over a year after introduction, traffic on the Hull–Liverpool route had increased by 100%!

Each train had four power cars, two at each end, and two trailers in the middle, one of which contained a griddle buffet. The intermediate power cars did not have driving cabs. The engines were 230bhp Leyland Albion six-cylinder horizontal diesel driving through heavy fluid couplings and SCG SE4 four-speed gearboxes. The end cab fronts had received professional design input to improve their forward appearance, resulting in stylish wrap-round windscreens. Internally the cars were furnished in similar style and comfort to the Scottish Class 126s.

Unfortunately, the diesel engines shut down frequently in service due to boiling coolant being discharged. Modifications to expand the volume of the cooling system around 1980 cured the problem.

Traffic lost to the new M62 motorway across the Pennines led to the buffet cars being withdrawn by 1975, reducing the trains to five-car sets. In the late 1970s the number of power cars in each train was reduced by taking off the engines and most transmission components on one car in each set. Further decline in passengers enabled the trains to be reduced to four cars.

In 1979 a recast of services led to these units being drafted to work between Hull and Manchester via Sheffield and the Hope Valley line. By this time they had been joined by '123s' from the WR, and became a joint fleet of four-car sets. By 1984, the spread of diesel locomotive-hauled services rendered the remaining Trans-Pennine DMUs redundant and the last was withdrawn that year.

Class	124 Trans-Pennine DMUs
Designed for	BR
Introduced	1960
Built by	BR Swindon
Wheel arrgt	1A-A1 (power cars)
Layout (outer cars)	duo-directional with one full-width cab
(intermediate power cars)	duo-directional with no driving cab
Engines	2 × Leyland Albion 902 230bhp diesels
Transmissions	2 × 4-speed SCG SE4 gearboxes; reversing final drives
Max speed	70mph
Coupling code	blue square
Seats	57, 48 (power cars); 18 (trailer buffets), 64 (trailer seconds)
Heating	Smith's oil-fired warm air heaters
Underframe	64.5ft
Weight in wo	40, 41 tons (power cars); 32 tons, 34 tons* (trailers)
Number built	51 vehicles
BR numbers	51951–84 (power cars); 59765–73, 59774–81* (trailers).

* Buffet cars.

Above: *A Trans-Pennine six-car unit arrives at Huddersfield on 10 July 1961 on a Hull to Liverpool Lime Street working. The third vehicle is a buffet-griddle car.* Author

Left: *The '124s' were later shortened by removal of the buffet cars. This view of a five-car formation leaving Leeds City for Liverpool in 1976 shows the wrap-round cab windscreens inserted in the fibreglass resin cab front. The sets were later reduced to four cars and some engines removed.* Author

The very last new type of 'first-generation' BR DMU was the Inter-City Class 123 which emerged from Swindon Works in 1963. These were built for South Wales to Birmingham and Portsmouth services. They were unique among BR DMUs in that they rode on modern bogies of the B.5 type (power cars) and B.4. The 10 four-car sets included five with buffet trailers. All sets were gangwayed throughout, including the cab ends, which enabled passengers to reach the buffet car when two sets were coupled together in multiple.

In other respects they were similar to the earlier Class 124 units, having bodies and underframes made up of fabricated steel pressings welded together as a structural box, and using buckeye couplings, oval-headed retractable buffers and Pullman-type gangways. Although, when introduced, they had four-digit route indicators, these were subsequently removed and replaced by combined electric marker lamps and tail lamps, as was done with most other DMU fleets.

In operation the '123s' were much better riding vehicles than previous designs of DMU, and deservedly popular, at least in their first decade or so. The sets gravitated to work outer suburban services out of London, the buffet cars having been withdrawn, and were then declared surplus in 1977 and stored briefly at Barry. However, the Eastern Region saw the '123s' as an opportunity to improve the Hull-based longer-distance DMU services and agreed to take them on. They were compatible with the Class

A Class 123 Inter-City DMU forming a Portsmouth-Cardiff service runs through St Denys on the approach to Southampton on 21 February 1967. Author

Class	123 Inter-City DMUs
Designed for	BR
Introduced	1963
Built by	BR Swindon
Wheel arrgt	1A-A1 (power cars)
Layout	duo-directional with one half-width cab
Engines	2 × Leyland Albion 902 230bhp diesels
Transmissions	2 × 4-speed SCG SE4 gearboxes; reversing final drives
Max speed	70mph
Coupling code	blue square
Seats	32, 56 (power cars); 32 (trailer buffets), 48 (trailer seconds)
Heating	Lucas oil-fired warm air heaters
Underframe	64.5ft
Weight in wo	41 tons 14cwt, 41 tons 9cwt (power cars); 31 tons, 32 tons 3cwt, 35 tons* (trailers)
Number built	40 vehicles
BR numbers	52086–105 (power cars); 59235–9, 59818–27, 59828–32* (trailers).

* Buffet cars.

124 Trans-Pennine fleet, which was being shifted to duties that would cover hourly services between Hull, Doncaster, Sheffield and Manchester via the Hope Valley. Thus the two classes were reformed as four-car sets, and were productively used until displaced in 1984/5 by locomotive-hauled trains.

Although one buffet car (No 59828) became a mess van for a short time, none of the Class 123 vehicles survives today.

CHAPTER 7: **BR DIESEL PARCELS CARS**

The GWR had set the scene for using single diesel railcars designed for carrying express parcels and capable of hauling one or two additional vans. BR followed suit with two basic designs of parcels car, all being versions of existing passenger DMU cars.

In 1958 three parcels cars were built by Cravens of Sheffield for service on the LM Region. These were followed in 1959 by two variants of parcels cars by the Gloucester Carriage & Wagon Company. Their uses included carrying mails and newspapers, and traffic on BR's Red Star Parcels service.

In the 1980s, several otherwise redundant passenger DMUs, mainly power cars, were converted for parcels operation. The impetus for this was the creation of a Parcels business sector within BR. This business actively promoted parcels and mail traffic. Additional and economic train capacity became urgent. In later years these units were replaced by locomotive-hauled trains, some push-pull, and the parcels DMUs were finally retired, mostly in the early 1990s.

Cravens Class 129 parcels DMUs

The design of the three Cravens parcels cars was based closely on the Class 105 passenger DMU, except that the parcels cars had a cab at each end. The side doors, through which parcels would be loaded and unloaded at station platforms, were standard guard's brake doors in pairs, as on the guard's van of a '105', except that there were three pairs of these doors on each side of a parcels car. The cars had normal full-width driving cabs with no gangways.

Traction was a pair of AEC 150bhp engines driving through standard mechanical transmissions. This enabled the cars to haul one trailer vehicle successfully. Two would be a strain!

Originally intended to couple with Derby 'lightweight' units in Cumbria, they were wired to be compatible with vehicles with the yellow diamond coupling code. In fact this was never used as the parcels cars ended up in the Birmingham area, so the Cravens cars had to remain separate on all services on which they worked. Delivered in lined Brunswick green with 'speed whiskers' on the cab fronts, they later received BR's corporate plain rail blue livery.

Withdrawn as surplus and non-standard in 1973, two of the cars had a period in departmental service. Two '129s' were broken up in 1975, but No 55997 lasted until 1986 before it met its end.

M55998 was one of three Craven parcels cars of Class 129; all worked on the London Midland Region. It was glimpsed at Birmingham New Street on 30 August 1958. Author

Classes	129 and 128 parcels DMUs	
Class	**129**	**128**
Designed for	BR	BR
Introduced	1958	1959
Built by	Cravens	Gloucester RC&W Co
Wheel arrgt	1A-A1 (power cars)	1A-A1 (power cars)
Layout	duo-directional with two full-width cabs	duo-directional with full-width** or two half-width cabs
Engines	2 × AEC 150bhp diesels*	2 × Leyland Albion 902 230bhp diesels
Transmissions	2 × Wilson 4-speed gearboxes; reversing final drives	2 × 4-speed SCG SE4 gearboxes; reversing final drives
Max speed	70mph	70mph
Coupling code	yellow diamond	blue square
Seats	none	none
Heating	Lucas	Smith's
Underframe	57.5ft	64.5ft
Weight in wo	30 tons	40,** 41 tons
Number built	3 vehicles	10 vehicles
BR numbers	55997–99	55987–96

* The '129s' were later fitted with Leyland 680 150bhp engines.
** Nos 55987–90 were non-gangwayed with full-width cabs; 55991–6 were gangwayed with half-width cabs.

Ten more parcels cars came from the Gloucester Carriage & Wagon Company in 1959, the first four for the LM Region and six for the Western. The LMR cars were non-gangwayed, but the WR vehicles had standard DMU gangways at each end. These vehicles were equipped with 230bhp Leyland Albion engines. This enabled them to haul up to two bogie vans with ease.

Externally the body shape followed the profile of the Gloucester-built passenger cars of Class 100, but with three pairs of recessed doors to access the van space. The guard's compartment was linked to the clear van space which was 55ft long and had wall racks for letters and small parcels, straps for restraining bicycles and a stowing point for a gangway cover plate for use when coupled to another gangwayed DMU. The gangways were, however, not compatible with the Pullman-type gangways on mark 1-hauled stock including the relevant BG vans. In later years some of the cars had their gangways removed and the cab fronts blanked off.

The '128s' were initially spread between the London end of the WR, the West Midlands, and the Manchester and Chester areas. By the 1980s they could be seen as far north as York and as far west as the Cambrian coast. Indeed, one was used to haul civil engineering trains during the period when Barmouth Bridge was banned to locomotives.

In the 1980s some of the vehicles received new Leyland TL11 diesel engines, common with the new 'Pacer' units, and these were recovered from the parcels cars when they were scrapped in 1990.

Liveries began with the standard lined dark green, then overall rail blue, a few with red-and-white side bands, and finally the attractive lined post-office red with yellow doors emblazoned with red wasp stripes when allocated to BR's Parcels business sector. The last was withdrawn in 1990. None is preserved.

Top: *The first four Gloucester parcels cars were non-gangwayed and had a central window. No M55987 was at Newton Heath depot on 20 April 1963 and displays its four-digit route indicator and small yellow warning panel.* Author

Above: *On 26 May 1990 a Gloucester parcels car with gangways removed leads a Class 114 conversion out of Hereford. Note how the exhausts from both engines are led up the cab front at one end of the car.* Peter Swift

Left: *Loading up in a bay platform at York in 1990 is a gangwayed parcels car also in Royal Mail red livery.* Author

Conversions from passenger DMUs

A surprising total of 283 otherwise redundant DMU vehicles were converted for use in BR's departmental stock and a further 73 worked for a time as parcels vehicles. Some of these vehicles destined for parcels work were given the full treatment of re-equipping the interiors and fitment of wide side doors. Others just had the seats taken out.

The following photographs only scratch the surface of the variety that appeared on parcels-carrying work in the 1970s and 1980s. The captions tell their stories.

Top right: *Some Class 116 power cars were coupled outside former locomotive-hauled GUV vehicles to form useful four-car parcels units.* Colour-Rail

Right: *A train of Class 114 vehicles, formed of one power-trailer twin and a second power car, work a parcels service approaching York from the south in 1987. These particular vehicles had not been modified with wide doors, so were restricted in the size of parcels they could carry other than in the guard's van.* Author

Below: *A more substantial conversion was undertaken on Class 127s to form parcels cars with wide roller-shutter doors on each side. This one in a special 'heritage' livery was at an open day at Carlisle Upperby depot in 1986. Note the Royal Mail stickers alongside the doors.* Author

When BR launched its 1955 Modernisation Plan, the Southern Region had already decided that it did not want to enter the market for diesel-mechanical multiple-units, which would be incompatible with both its operations policy and its technical expertise. The SR had already established the largest network of electric railways in the UK. It wanted to use its current technical knowledge and experience in the development of a new range of diesel multiple-unit trains that would use as far as possible components that were standard with its existing electric rolling stock, particularly that which was being designed and built in part to BR standard designs.

The SR managed to persuade BR HQ that it could go its own way, and thus, in close collaboration with the English Electric Company which was its main supplier of proven electric traction equipment, the SR ordered and built a fleet of diesel-electric multiple-units. These used standard carriage underframes and bogies from the EMU range, standard carriage bodies (except for the Hastings units) and standard traction motors and control equipment. Indeed the only novelty in them was the power unit. This was a floor-standing, vertical four-cylinder diesel coupled to a DC generator with tappings for train heat, light and control supply. The engine cylinders were 10in diameter with a 12in piston stroke and were fed pressurised air through a turbocharger. At 500bhp this engine was regarded initially as adequate for powering a two- or three-coach unit; two would be used in a six-car set.

Advantages of this arrangement included the ease of access of the engine for maintenance, its innate reliability and the expectation that engines would last a lot longer between overhauls than the bus-type engines used on diesel mechanical units. The use of standard electrical equipment simplified storekeeping and purchasing and, because it was already well-developed technically, would support the overall reliability of the trains.

There were inherent disadvantages, of course, chief among them being the loss of passenger space due to the above-floor placement of the power unit in the vehicle. Also, because the power unit was to be located on the carriage longitudinal centre-line for balance, there was insufficient room to run a corridor past it. Thus the units would need to be non-gangwayed at the outer ends. Also, the noise and vibrations from the heavy power unit could disturb passengers riding in the power cars. The heavy weight of the power unit was met by using a non-motored motor bogie to carry the front of each power car, the motored bogie being at the back.

The range of units produced with this arrangement included the 8ft-wide Hastings sets and two- and three-car sets for Hampshire, Berkshire and Sussex. Engineers in Northern Ireland were appreciative of the success of these units in BR traffic, and developed for UTA and NIR three further classes based on the principle, all using the well-established EE 4SRKT power unit for traction. The first of these was put into service from 1966 on the Belfast–Londonderry line via Coleraine. They were followed in 1974 by the very successful Class 80 units, and in 1985 by nine more modern ones, but using second-hand electrical equipment.

The diesel-electric multiple-units were rugged, long-lasting trains. On BR the last few survived until replaced in 2003/4 by new Class 170 Turbostars. On NIR a few Class 80 sets and all the Class 450s are still in service at the time of writing (2010).

The Southern Region rarely used half-measures! With two six-car DEMU sets in multiple, this 12-car Hastings to London Charing Cross train represents one of the longest DMUs regularly to run on BR. Class 203 unit 1033 leads '202' buffet unit 1013 on an Up working passing through Hither Green on 20 May 1961. Author

Classes	201–203 DEMUs
Designed for	BR
Introduced	1957
Built by	BR Eastleigh*
Wheel arrgt	2-Bo (power cars)
Layout	six-car sets gangwayed internally
Power unit	English Electric 4SRKT four-cylinder upright 500bhp diesel engine and EE generator
Traction motors	2 × EE507 dc
Max speed	90mph
Coupling code	SR DEMU
Seats	Class 201: 22 (power cars); 52, 42 (trailers); Class 202, 203: 30 (power cars); 48, 56, 60 (trailer cars); 21 (buffet cars)
Heating	electric
Underframe	57ft (Class 201); 63.5ft (Classes 202, 203)
Weight in wo	power cars: 54 tons 2cwt ('201'), 55 tons ('202', '203'); trailers: 29, 30, 32 tons
Number built	'201': 7 units; '202': 9 units; '203': 7 units
Set numbers	'201': 1001–7; '202': 1011–9; '203': 1031–7.

*Underframes were built at Ashford.

When new carriages were proposed in 1956 to enable diesel locomotives to replace steam on London to Hastings services, operators knew they could just squeeze a 12-coach train and a diesel locomotive in the platforms at Charing Cross if the carriages were on standard suburban 57ft-long underframes. The first batch of these underframes was being built at Ashford Works when came the decision to build DEMUs instead. Happily, 12 MU carriages on 63ft 6in underframes would also fit the platforms. So the short underframes were used up in the first seven six-car 'Hastings' DEMUs (Class 201), and all later DEMUs on BR/SR were built on the standard BR mark 1 type of longer underframe.

Because of tight clearances in the Hastings line tunnels, the 'Hastings' DEMUs were built with flat-sided, 8ft 2in-wide coaches. Peak trains would run with two six-car units which would be uncoupled on arrival at Tunbridge Wells; the leading buffet set would run faster to Hastings, the second non-buffet unit following it to call at all stations. Sixteen non-buffet sets were built from 1957, of which the last nine (Class 202) were on long underframes. The seven sets with buffets (Class 203) came out in 1958. The longer underframes enabled an extra compartment or seating bay to be included.

When the Bexhill West branch closed, three '201s' were disbanded and reformed to make up part of the Class 206 units (see page 66). Buffet cars were withdrawn in later years and the affected sets reduced to five cars by 1980.

The 'Hastings' DEMUs performed reliably through to electrification of the Charing Cross–Hastings route in 1986, by which time body corrosion was setting in and scrapping was perhaps inevitable.

One unit is preserved and registered for main line use as unit 1001. Two vehicles became part of departmental stock, former buffet car S60755 surviving at the time of writing in good condition as a green-painted saloon carrying the name *Caroline*.

Top left: *Long-underframe power cars were identifiable from the four seating bays between the guard's compartment and the inner end door; the '201' cars had just three bays. Class 203 unit No 1031 is at the rear of a 12-car formation leaving Tunbridge Wells Central for Hastings in 1985.* Author

Below: *A remarkable survivor was the preserved 'Hastings' unit given the set number 1001 but in fact all on long underframes. This unit was frequently hired out to train operators to cover stock shortages, made up of three, four or five coaches, for example on 20 March 2003 when it was at Hastings on a Connex working from Ashford.* Author

For local services in Hampshire, BR/SR built at Eastleigh 18 two-car DEMUs based on the BR standard 9ft 3in-wide suburban carriage design but with 63ft 6in-long underframes. They were not gangwayed. The power cars had five second-class seating bays with slam doors to each bay. The driving trailers had a similar layout at the inner end; there were two toilets in the middle, then two first-class compartments with a short corridor linking them to a toilet, then a second-class compartment with no corridor (this later became a luggage compartment). Power equipment was standard with the 'Hastings ' power cars.

So successful was the interval service provided by these trains (initially classified 2H) that overcrowding was common within weeks! Each unit was quickly strengthened with a third vehicle, a 104-seat second-class intermediate trailer. New 4SRKT diesel engines were fitted, uprated to 600bhp to maintain performance. The displaced 500bhp engines went into new-build 'Hastings' units. All the 'Hampshire' units were later classified '205'. A batch of four two-car units was then built for the Ashford–Hastings line. These became Class 204. Then in 1962 came the seven three-car 'Berkshire' units for Reading–Salisbury services which had longer brake vans and consequently 10 fewer second-class seats.

Three Class 205 sets were soon reduced to two cars to help them cope with the inclines on the Winchester–Alton line. In 1979 all remaining two-car units were strengthened to three cars by inserting driving trailers from some '205s' that in turn had received third-hand ex-2EPB driving trailers from withdrawn Class 206 sets (page 66), and became a new Class 204.

Classes	204 and 205 DEMUs
Designed for	BR
Introduced	1957
Built by	BR Eastleigh*
Wheel arrgt	2-Bo (power cars)
Layout	three-car sets non-gangwayed**
Power unit	English Electric 4SRKT four-cylinder upright 600bhp diesel engine and EE generator
Traction motors	2 × EE507 dc
Max speed	75mph***
Coupling code	SR DEMU
Seats	power cars: 52, 42#; intermediate trailer cars (Class 205 only): 104; driving trailer cars: 63
Heating	electric
Underframe	63.5ft
Weight in wo	power cars: 56 tons; trailers: 30, 32 tons
Number built	'205': 29 units; '204': 4 units
Set numbers	'205': 1101–18, 1123–26; 1127–33#; '204': 1119–22/1401–4##.

*   Underframes were built at Ashford.
**   Class 204 were two-car units with no intermediate trailer.
*** For a time in 1961–62 some '205s' were re-geared for 90mph but suffered from low acceleration and low-speed overloads; they were quickly reverted to standard.
#   'Berkshire' units.
Three of the four later '204s' were reformed '205' units.

After closures or electrification of the routes in Hampshire frequented by these units, several moved to work for many years on Ashford–Hastings, East Grinstead and Uckfield services; the last few survived in active service to December 2004. Nine sets have been saved for preservation.

Above left: Class 205 'Hampshire' three-car set No 1107 energetically leaves Medstead & Four Marks on a Southampton Terminus to Alton working in May 1966. G. H. Hunt/Colour-Rail

Bottom: Class 205 'Berkshire' unit No 1133 calls at Westbury on 26 March 1977 with the 11.15 from Bristol Temple Meads to Portsmouth Harbour. The power car has a longer guard's brake van than the 'Hampshire' variety which leaves room for only four seating bays instead of five. Brian Morrison

BR Class 206 DEMUs

The Southern Region's wisdom of adopting the DEMU principle so that its diesel multiple-units could use established EMU technology is shown in the creation in 1964 of the six Class 206 units. These were formed after some of the 'Hastings' Class 201 units were disbanded following closure of the Bexhill West branch. Each three-car Class 206 unit consisted of a Class 201 power car and a Class 201 standard-class trailer, coupled to a standard-class driving trailer from a BR suburban Class 416 EMU. The EMU driving controls needed replacement by DEMU control system. The driving trailer vehicle was 9ft 3in wide. Compared with the 8ft 2in body-width of the former Class 201 vehicles, the driving trailer looked large and bulbous. Thus the units gained the nickname 'tadpoles'. The '206s' spent most of their life working the cross-country line between Tonbridge and Reading via Redhill and Guildford.

All BR/SR DEMUs were initially painted BR carriage green, a colour reminiscent of, but darker than, the old Southern malachite green. From the mid-1960s small yellow warning panels were applied to cab fronts, and then, on those with brake vans, an inverted black triangle was added to help station staff know at which end was the brake van. BR/SR green gave way to rail blue at overhauls undertaken from 1966. Later, probably from 1968 in common with the Bournemouth line express EMUs, the 'Hastings' and 'tadpole' DEMUs received blue-and-grey livery, which suited them far better than any plain colour.

The 'tadpoles' had to move in 1979 (when Western Region-allocated Class 119 DMUs were drafted to the Reading–Gatwick service) and found work in the SR's Central Division including on the Uckfield and Ashford–Hastings lines. The last Class 206 unit was withdrawn in 1987.

Class	206 DEMUs
Designed for	BR
Introduced	1964*
Built by	BR Eastleigh
Wheel arrgt	2-Bo (power cars)
Layout	three-car sets gangwayed internally
Power unit	English Electric 4SRKT four-cylinder upright 500bhp diesel engine and EE generator
Traction motors	2 × EE507 dc
Max speed	90mph
Coupling code	SR DEMU
Seats	power cars: 22; intermediate trailer cars: 52; driving trailer cars: 66
Heating	electric
Underframe	57ft
Weight in wo	power cars: 54 tons 2cwt; trailers: 29, 30 tons
Number formed	6 units
Set numbers	1201–6**.

*   Reformed from two Class 201 vehicles with a Class 416 driving trailer.
** Some units were later renumbered in 13XX series, and later still in formal BR style as 206 10X.

The so-called 'tadpole' units were formed of two 'Hastings' short-underframe vehicles with a non-corridor driving trailer from a 2EPB EMU. No 1204 stands at Eastleigh Works after overhaul in 1969. They worked mainly between Reading and Tonbridge. Author

Class	207 DEMUs
Designed for	BR
Introduced	1962
Built by	BR Eastleigh*
Wheel arrgt	2-Bo (power cars)
Layout	three-car sets non-gangwayed**
Power unit	English Electric 4SRKT four-cylinder upright 600bhp diesel engine and EE generator
Traction motors	2 × EE507 dc
Max speed	75mph
Coupling code	SR DEMU
Seats	power cars: 42; intermediate trailer cars 66, driving trailer cars: 76
Heating	electric
Underframe	64ft
Weight in wo	power cars: 56 tons; trailers: 31, 32 tons
Number built	19 units
Set numbers	1301–19.

*   Underframes were built at Ashford.
** Some sets were later modified with internal gangways.

When it was planned to eliminate steam traction from the Oxted group of lines in the Central Division, more three-car diesel-electric units were ordered. To get trains through the narrower tunnels in the Tunbridge Wells area, a narrower body-width of 8ft 6in was selected, enabling the BR standard curved body profile and standard doors and fittings to be used. The cab fronts and slam doors were formed in fibreglass resin, the multiple working jumper cables and brake hoses being secured in recesses below the windscreens. The seating layout was different: first class was in the intermediate trailer car.

On the original 'Hampshire' DEMUs the ride in the power car was hard and unyielding during acceleration and braking. Experiments to improve the bogie ride began in 1960 with modifications to the length and angle of bolster swing links and the width of the spring planks. The bogies for the 'Oxted' units were built when the bogie improvement process had reached mark 3. The final mark 4 version that was applied to other DEMUs in retrospect, included provision of anti-roll bars, and vertical and lateral hydraulic damping, making a big improvement.

The 19 Class 207 units performed well and spent most of their lives in the areas for which they were designed, adding the non-electrified south Kent routes to their sphere of operation. When the Oxted route to London was electrified by BR, some of the '207s' went to work between Tonbridge, Redhill and Reading. Others spent a time working between Reading and Basingstoke. All the remaining ones ended up on Sussex and Kent services until the last was withdrawn in 2004. Three complete units and a couple of odd vehicles are preserved, on the Spa Valley Railway, the East Lancashire Railway and on the Swindon & Cricklade Railway (a two-car unit).

Top left: *Class 207 'Oxted' unit No 1314 enters Eridge on a Tunbridge Wells to Eastbourne service in May 1965. These units had narrower bodies to fit tight tunnels bequeathed by the South Eastern Railway.* Bruce Nathan/Colour-Rail

Below: *Although Network SouthEast was not keen on six-figure set numbers, it did apply them to DEMUs to avoid clashing with EMU numbers. No 207 001 sits patiently at Basingstoke in 1991 on a service for Reading.* Author

UTA Class 70 DEMUs

Possibly because of the unreliability of Ulster Transport Authority's underfloor-engined diesel railcars, perhaps because their main advocate among UTA's engineers had retired, or ostensibly because UTA wanted more heavy railcars that could pull freight trains, the pattern of diesel trains in Northern Ireland changed completely from 1966. Seven diesel-electric railcars had been ordered, using the DEMU principle so successfully introduced on BR's Southern Region from 1957. The vehicle bodies were built at Belfast Duncrue Street Works, and the trailer cars were rebuilds of early LMS/NCC carriages, even older ones than those converted for the MPD programme (see page 29). An eighth power car followed later.

Underframes, bogies and power equipment were imported from the English Electric Company. Two six-car express sets were assembled for the Belfast–Coleraine–Londonderry route. These were gangwayed between vehicles, but not at the outer ends of the power cars because of the presence of the above-floor power unit behind each driving cab. Two three-car units were also put together, each with a gangwayed driving trailer at the non-powered end. These worked mainly on the Belfast–Larne route.

The units proved to be reliable, if heavy and a bit bouncy in service. For a couple of years towards 1970 a set was used on the Belfast–Dublin 'Enterprise' trains. Additional driving trailers were converted and proved useful when carryings on the Derry road declined and three-car units became the norm. The trains were liveried in the standard UTA/Northern Ireland Railways dark red and oyster grey at the start, then later they appeared in the royal blue-and-maroon style. One set in the early 1980s received a garish multi-coloured livery for the Larne boat train service.

Class	70 DEMUs
Designed for	UTA
Introduced	1966
Built by	UTA Duncrue Street
Wheel arrgt	2-Bo (power cars)
Layout	six-car sets gangwayed internally; three-car sets gangwayed internally and through driving trailers
Power unit	English Electric 4SRKT four-cylinder upright 550bhp diesel engine and EE generator
Traction motors	2 × EE538 dc
Max speed	70mph
Coupling code	none
Seats	power cars: 44; trailer cars: various
Heating	electric
Underframe	63ft
Weight in wo	power cars: 56 tons; trailers: 31, 32 tons
Number built	8 power cars, 18 trailer cars*
Vehicle numbers	power cars: 71–8; trailer cars: 548, 550 (buffet cars), 701–3, 711–2, 721–5; later additions: 554, 713–4, 726–8.

* Rebuilt from LMS/NCC carriages.

These robust but increasingly unpopular units were replaced in the mid-1980s when the Class 450 three-car units arrived in Northern Ireland (see page 70). None is preserved. Their electric traction equipment, however, lives on in the Class 450 units.

Right: *In 1967, a year after its introduction, a Class 70 DEMU train, led by railcar No 72, awaits departure for Belfast York Road from Londonderry Waterside. These vehicles introduced diesel-electric multiple-units to Northern Ireland which became the norm there for the next four decades.* Colour-Rail

Below: *Two Class 70 three-car sets await their next duties at Belfast York Road in October 1984. No 72 (left) was repainted in a special livery for the Belfast–Larne boat trains that connected with the Stranraer ferries. A set of BR mark 1 coaches was similarly painted for the onwards connection to Glasgow.* Author

Class 70 power car names	
71	River Bush
72	River Foyle
73	River Roe
74	River Lagan
75	River Maine
76	River Inver
77	River Braid
78	River Bann

By the early 1970s the mixed fleet of DMUs on NIR were ageing and there grew a pressing need to replace them. Satisfied with the performance of the Class 70 DEMUs, NIR ordered more DEMUs, this time from BREL in England, the first batch being four three-car sets and five twin-units. Their design adapted the British Rail mark 2b carriage design to suit their Irish duties. Each unit had one power car with a full-width driving cab. The intermediate trailer cars were basically mark 2b standard open vehicles. The driving trailers were similar, but with a half-width driving cab at the outer end which was gangwayed. Two units coupled back-to-back could enable passengers to access all vehicles in the train. Power car bodies were mounted on BR mark 1-type underframes, carried on mark 6 motor bogies; the leading bogie was non-motored and the inner bogie was motored. The 4SRKT engine was rated at 560bhp. Compared with the BR/SR 'Hampshire' units, the higher torque of the EE538 motors gave the Class 80 sets noticeably higher acceleration from stops. Trailer cars rode on B.5 bogies.

Internally the '80s' were similar to BR mark 2 stock except that their seating was higher-density. The brighter interiors and better ride made them superior for passengers than the BR DEMUs.

These units arrived in Northern Ireland in 1974, and a further 13 three-car sets came in 1977. They covered a high proportion of NIR services. In 1987 three three-car units were loaned to CIÉ for services on the Maynooth, Greystones and Cobh lines, but were returned to NIR in late 1990.

Class	80 DEMUs
Designed for	NIR
Introduced	1974
Built by	BREL Derby
Wheel arrgt	2-Bo (power cars)
Layout	power cars full-width cab at outer end; all other cars gangwayed both ends
Power unit	English Electric 4SRKT four-cylinder upright 560bhp diesel engine and EE generator
Traction motors	2 × EE538 dc
Max speed	70mph
Coupling code	none
Seats	power cars: 45; trailer cars: 75, 81
Heating	electric
Underframe	66ft
Weight in wo	power cars: 62 tons; trailers: 28, 32 tons 10cwt
Number built	22 power cars; 26 driving trailer cars;* 20 intermediate trailers**
NIR numbers	power cars: 67–9, 81–99; driving trailer cars: 731–56; intermediate trailers: 761–80
Translink Nos***	8067–9, 8081–99; 8731–56; 8761–80.

*   Three were rebuilt from BR mark 2c carriages.
**   Six were conversions from BR mark 2b carriages.
***   Not all vehicles carried Translink numbers.

All were supposed to be replaced by the Class 3000 CAF-built units introduced in 2004, but such was traffic growth on NIR that three four-car trains of Class 80 vehicles have had to be assembled and refurbished for 21st-century services on the Larne line! These old units should finally disappear when the Class 4000 DMUs are delivered, due in 2011.

Top left: *The mainstay of NIR services for 30 years from 1974 were the Class 80 DEMUs, most of which were three-car formations like this one, seen leaving Adelaide on a Lisburn to Belfast Central working on 16 May 1988.* Author

Below: *The driving trailer end of a NIR DEMU was gangwayed so that the conductor could pass through sets coupled correctly together. This one is calling at Lisburn on a service from Portadown to Belfast on 2 September 1984.* Author

NIR Class 450 DEMUs

The Class 450 DEMUs were built by BREL in England and began to arrive in Northern Ireland in 1985. They were to replace the Class 70 DEMUs, of which the trailer cars were by then very old, and the power cars outmoded. The design of the Class 450 was intelligently conceived to keep down the price. Each vehicle has a new body based on that used on the British Rail Class 150 DMU (see page 79) and '317' and '455' EMUs. The bodies rest on second-hand BR mark 1 carriage underframes and thus sit somewhat higher than BR units which have integral underframes, the Irish loading gauge being able to accommodate this. As on the Class 80 units, the power cars use mark 6 bogies and the trailer cars B.5s.

Eight of the nine power cars inherited power units from withdrawn Class 70s, the ninth getting one from withdrawn Class 80 No 88. The other electric traction equipment also came from earlier NIR DEMUs. As with other Irish DEMUs, the power cars are non-gangwayed at the outer ends but all other carriage ends have gangways.

The Class 450 units, named after castles in the province, were split operationally between the Larne route and the Portadown–Belfast–Bangor line. After inauguration of the Dargan Bridge in Belfast which linked the network together in 1992, they appeared on services almost everywhere on the NIR system, turn and turn about with the Class 80s. More recently, since the Class 3000 DMUs took over the longer distance services, the 'Castle' class is concentrated more on Belfast suburban work, and on the Larne and Portrush lines.

Replacement of the '450s' is now in sight at the time of writing in 2010. While a comprehensive refurbishment of the passenger accommodation is improving the interiors of these units, better to complement the new CAF-built units, when the new Class 4000 DMUs are in service the 'Castles' will be displaced.

Class	450 DEMUs
Designed for	NIR
Introduced	1985
Built by	BREL Derby and York
Wheel arrgt	2-Bo (power cars)
Layout	power cars full-width cab at outer end; all other cars gangwayed both ends
Power unit	English Electric 4SRKT four-cylinder upright 550bhp*diesel engine and EE generator
Traction motors	2 × EE538 dc
Max speed	70mph
Coupling code	none
Seats**	power cars: 41; trailer cars: 75, 85
Heating	electric
Underframe	66ft 6in
Weight in wo	power cars: 62 tons; trailers: 30 tons 8cwt, 32 tons 8cwt
Number built	9 three-car units
NIR numbers	power cars: 451–9; driving trailer cars: 781–9; intermediate trailers: 791–9
Translink numbers	8451–9, 8781–9; 8791–9.

*No 457 had 560bhp engine from car 88.
**Includes a few tip-up seats.

Right: *The 'Castle' class DEMUs of NIR utilised second-hand BR mark 1 carriage underframes and NIR traction equipment, with new BREL bodies and B.5 and mark 6 bogies. Power car 459 leads the normal three-car formation on a Belfast suburban service calling at Adelaide station on 16 May 1988.* Author

Below: *The '450' class also had gangwayed driving trailer coaches, as on this one ready to leave Belfast Great Victoria Street with the 15.55 for Larne Town on 6 December 1996.* Author

Class 450	power car names
8451	Belfast Castle
8452	Olderfleet Castle
8453	Moiry Castle
8454	Carrickfergus Castle
8455	Galgorm Castle
8456	Gosford Castle
8457	Bangor Castle
8458	Antrim Castle
8459	Killyleagh Castle

This chapter brings to a close the story of the 'first-generation' diesel multiple-unit types. Electrification of the west coast main line between London and Birmingham and Manchester required diversion of most longer-distance trains to alternative routes. While this was to a degree acceptable using diesel locomotives on the Western Region's Birmingham–Paddington line and LM Region's Manchester Central–St Pancras route, the resultant extended journey times would be a marketing disaster for urgent business travellers whose loyalty BR wished to retain.

Having witnessed in the late 1950s the apparent success of the Trans-Europ Express diesel trains on the continent, BR proposed a group of luxury trains designed specifically for the morning business services from Birmingham and Manchester to London, and for the evening peak return services. The result was the 'blue Pullman' group of diesel-electric units.

In their original form they were not strictly multiple-units as they had no need to operate in multiple and were therefore not so equipped. A later modification changed that.

The new sets were route-specific in their length and layout. The Manchester Central–London St Pancras line required an all-first-class train of six Pullman coaches. For the Western Region two routes were planned, the one from Birmingham and also one between Bristol and London. Eight-car trains were specified for these, and with two-class accommodation.

Each power unit had a 1,000bhp MAN 12-cylinder diesel Vee-engine driving a GEC dc generator. The four traction motors for each end of a unit could not all be under the power car for reasons of excess weight. So under the power car were two motors on the inner bogie, the other two motors being fitted to the leading bogie of the adjacent passenger vehicle. Bogies were of the Swiss Schlieren design, which had a good reputation when used under long, hauled carriages on good Swiss track. When fitted with motors which drove opposite ends of the two adjacent axles and carrying shorter carriage bodies with different dynamics the bogies did not perform well. The ride was improved with adjustment, but was never as good as was perceived on the continent.

Introduced in 1959, the diesel Pullmans were admired for their strikingly handsome blue-and-white livery. The six-car sets bore the legend 'Midland Pullman', but the WR sets, being common in use between two routes, were simply labelled 'Pullman'.

When the west coast main line electrified train service had become established between London and Manchester, the Midland Pullman diesel sets and that running between Birmingham and Paddington were no longer required on those routes. The WR was able to use its surplus eight-car train to replace locomotive-hauled stock on the 'South Wales Pullman' services. The two six-car units were transferred from the LMR to the WR to take up the 'Bristol Pullman' roster. Receiving multiple working jumper cables and hoses for this duty, they were able to run as a pair in a 12-car formation on this busy, prestige route. Soon after this, in 1967, they were repainted in a reverse of BR's corporate blue-and-grey livery; most observers regretted the demise of the original livery.

The diesel Pullmans did not even stay in service long enough to be displaced by BR's high speed diesel trains (HSTs). On placement of new BR mark 2 coaches in WR main line service, the 'blue Pullmans' were almost summarily withdrawn as outmoded in 1973, and were later scrapped.

An eight-car diesel Pullman leaves Twerton tunnel on a Paddington–Swansea working in April 1973. This was the final livery borne by all these sets before their withdrawal in 1973. C. G. Maggs/Colour-Rail

Six-car diesel Pullman units

Class	6-car Pullman
Designed for	BR
Introduced	1959
Built by	Metro-Cammell
Wheel arrgt	2-Bo (power cars) + Bo-2 (adjacent vehicles)
Layout	power cars full-width cab at outer end; all other cars gangwayed both ends
Power units (2)	MAN L12V18/21S 12-cylinder Vee 1,000bhp diesel engine and GEC generator
Traction motors (8)	GEC dc frame-mounted
Max speed	90mph
Coupling code	none*
Seats	power cars: 12; motor cars: 18; trailer cars 36; all first class
	power cars: 18; motor cars: 27; trailer cars 36*
Heating	electric, with full air-conditioning
Underframe	65ft 6in
Weight in wo	power cars: 67 tons 10cwt; motor cars: 49; trailer cars: 33 tons
Number built	4 power cars; 4 motor cars; 4 trailers
BR numbers	power cars: 60090–3; motor cars: 60730–3; trailers 60740–3.

* These two six-car units were converted to run in multiple in 1967, and re-seated to first and second classes.

Emerging from Metro-Cammell's Washwood Heath factory in Birmingham in 1959, the first 'Midland Pullman' set created a sensation. Everything on it was new, from the handsome blue-and-white livery to modern interiors to the use of full air-conditioning. Nothing quite like it had been seen on Britain's railways before. The train's 90mph top speed coupled with a high power/weight ratio enabled usefully quicker journey times such as 83 minutes for the 99 miles from St Pancras to Leicester.

Each end car was a streamlined power car with some passenger accommodation; forward of that was the guard's compartment, and then the power compartment just behind the driver's cab. The MAN power unit stood centrally on the vehicle floor. This was not a problem because it was never envisaged that they would ever be worked in multiple, and so there were no end gangways to these units. The kitchen car with its one motor bogie was behind the power car, and that too had a seating area. There were two parlour cars in the middle of the train, then another motor/kitchen car and then the rear power car. Each train half was a mirror-image of the other. All seats were in formation of 2+1 across an offset central gangway, grouped round tables face-to-face. The notable difference from

older Pullman cars was the modern design of the seating, and of the train interior in total. All cars were air-conditioned, a first for BR.

Two complete six-car sets were supplied for the Manchester Central–London St Pancras route, one being required as a maintenance and overhaul back-up for the other. Normally the sets were not split, though the author recalls once seeing a half-set heading round the Derby Chaddesden Sidings area en route to London.

With completion of the wcml electrification in 1966, the two six-car units were transferred to the Western Region for the 'Bristol Pullman' service. This became very successful such that a 12-car formation was needed. The two six-car sets therefore received multiple working connections on their cab fronts from 1967.

Above: *The 'Midland Pullman' initially terminated at Leicester London Road during its fill-in return run from London St Pancras between the morning and evening peak workings between Manchester and London. This was Leicester on 5 September 1960.* Author

Right: *The need to expand the 'Bristol Pullman' service after the 'Midland Pullman' sets had reached the WR necessitated running two six-car units in multiple. This power car, caught by the camera at Bath Spa in June 1967, shows off its new jumper cables.* Colour-Rail

One of the Western Region's eight-car sets rests at Tyseley depot on Sunday 29 April 1962. Author

Class	8-car Pullman
Designed for	BR
Introduced	1959
Built by	Metro-Cammell
Wheel arrgt	2-Bo (power cars) + Bo-2 (adjacent vehicles)
Layout	power cars full-width cab at outer end; all other cars gangwayed both ends
Power units (2)	MAN L12V18/21S 12-cylinder Vee 1,000bhp diesel engine and GEC generator
Traction motors (8)	GEC dc frame-mounted
Max speed	90mph
Coupling code	none
Seats	power cars: 18; motor cars: 42; trailer cars 18, 36
Heating	electric, with full air-conditioning
Underframe	65ft 6in
Weight in wo	power cars: 67 tons 10cwt; motor cars: 49 tons; trailer cars: 33, 36 tons
Number built	6 power cars; 6 motor cars; 12 trailers
BR numbers	power cars: 60094–9; motor cars: 60644–9; trailers 60734–9, 60744–9.

For the Western Region business trains from Birmingham and Bristol to London Paddington three eight-car units were supplied in a two-class configuration. Second-class seating was also in a 2+1 layout. The power cars and the adjoining parlour cars (which were motored) were second class, then followed a kitchen vehicle and then a first-class parlour car; the second half of the train was the same but the other way round.

Working on the somewhat easier gradients of the former GWR main lines, the diesel Pullman units broke records for fast journey times. The fastest was later in their life when a timing was introduced of 73 minutes for the 93 miles from Paddington to Chippenham, a creditable start-to-stop average speed of 77.3mph.

From 1967 when the services were revised, the eight-car sets went over to work the twice-daily 'South Wales Pullman' services between Swansea and Paddington. At that time they received the new BR corporate Pullman livery of rail grey for the bodies and a wide rail blue band along the window area. Because the outline of the units was always quite modern in shape, they looked quite sharp in the new livery, though there were always dissenting voices!

The author worked in Cardiff for a couple of years and sampled these trains on business trips to Reading and London. While the ambience and catering were excellent, the ride was not good; the tendency to jerk and

bounce was at times unpleasant; this mismatch between a continental bogie design and UK carriages and track was never fully resolved.

One eight-car unit was held as a spare for all five 'blue Pullman' sets, a more economic arrangement than had applied when the sets were allocated to two different regions. All however had been withdrawn from service by the end of 1973 and no vehicle from this group is preserved.

CHAPTER 10: 'PACER' SERIES TWO-AXLE DMUS

Three Class 142 'Pacer' units, all decked out in the new orange livery of Greater Manchester Passenger Transport Executive, form suburban trains in Manchester Piccadilly station on 26 April 1986. Author

By the end of the 1970s BR was energetically considering with what to begin replacing the oldest 'first-generation' DMUs which were already 20 years old. The concept of using relatively low-powered bus engines to move heavy carriages around the country at up to 70mph had proved costly in engineering terms. Overhaul lives of diesel engines and gearboxes in particular were much shorter on average than had originally been anticipated. As engines aged, break-ups became more frequent. The presence of floor hatches designed to help maintenance staff access the tops of diesel engines had a hazardous side: when a connecting rod burst out through a crankcase it was possible for the flailing metal to break through the floor hatch into the passenger compartment; the resultant crankcase explosion could scorch and justifiably frighten passengers. Something more robust was needed, but not necessarily so robust and expensive as the English Electric engines in the BR Southern Region and NIR DEMUs.

BR initiated two lines of experiment. These are described in more detail on pages 120-21. In brief, there was a development of the Research Department's innovation of high speed freight vehicles to evolve a two-axle lightweight diesel railcar using bus body components, and in parallel a trial of a modern DEMU using standard BR EMU vehicles as a basis. The latter was not pursued beyond two prototypes but the two-axle railbus idea led to a range of DMUs being built to that principle.

The carriage bodies were constructed from standard Leyland National bus parts, but with the passenger access doors strengthened to withstand the pressure pulses generated by passing trains. Underframes and suspensions were similar to those used on the '140', being linear descendants from BR Research's high speed freight vehicle HSFV1. The 'Pacers' have flexible coil spring suspensions with the wheelsets allowed considerable freedom of movement in the lateral plane but suitably constrained from resonant hunting by hydraulic damping, a principle eagerly and quickly copied by railways in Hungary and Czechoslovakia for their rural diesel railcars.

The 'Pacers' had bus bench-type seating, originally arranged in a 3+2 layout; this has mostly been replaced in more recent years by modern individual seating as vehicles have been refurbished for different franchisees. Other decoration is plastic but minimal, usually subsequently refurbished by painting. Ventilation is by hopper windows. The units are gangwayed internally. Classes 141 to 143 are of two-car

formation and Class 144 includes 10 units of a three-car type. Each twin unit has one toilet at the inner end of one car. Passenger access is through three pairs of twin-leaf doors on each side of each two-car unit. The Class 142 to 144 bodies were built wider than the '140' and '141' types to take better advantage of the BR loading gauge and enable capacity or comfort to be enhanced.

Each car was supplied with one Leyland 205bhp horizontal diesel engine driving through a Voith hydraulic torque converter and cardan shaft to one axle. As these are lightweight vehicles of 25 tons maximum weight, in low adhesion rail conditions drivers need to be careful when braking to avoid sliding past stopping points. Sometimes slippery rails can cause difficulty in restarting from stations in leafy areas.

The ride of these two-axle vehicles is more sensitive to track conditions than if they were bogie vehicles. On continuous welded rail (CWR) a 'Pacer' can give a pleasantly stable ride, but jointed track and points and crossings cause them to dip into the rail joints. Side sway is exaggerated by lateral track imperfections. On sharply-curved routes their long vehicle wheelbase can cause high-pitched wheel tread squealing, eased when the track has adequate rail lubrication on curves. The squealing is a cause of premature wheel disc cracking. This has been cured by bonding damping material to the wheel discs, which cuts down the noise.

The railbus units operate mostly in the north of England around and between the Liverpool, Manchester, Leeds, Sheffield and Tyneside conurbations, and in the South Wales valleys and the West Country. They are technically the least reliable of the second-generation DMUs, though as experience in overcoming their faults has continued to be shared, franchisees' maintenance teams have lifted most of the units' reliability issues out of the public's consciousness.

While the 'Pacers' are the nation's least popular DMUs today, on account of their less comfortable riding characteristics and draughtiness, replacements for them are still a distant aspiration at the time of writing in 2010.

Following the technically successful trials of the Class 140 prototype (see page 120) BR ordered from Leyland Motors 20 two-car two-axle DMUs for services in the West Yorkshire PTE area. These were similar to the '140' except that the units were only gangwayed internally, the outer ends having full-width flat fronts, an improvement to their appearance; body width using standard bus body parts was 2.5 metres, narrower than railway standard. West Yorkshire had the units painted in a rather weak livery of cream and light green. Among design features that had clearly not been fully resolved from operation of the prototype was the problem of reliability of the use of calliper- operated brakes. Cables sometimes chafed against nearby steel structural members, and there were weaknesses in the door mechanisms. Operational reliability did not reach expected levels.

In 1984 a Class 141 unit was demonstrated to councillors and officials of Greater Manchester and its PTE. When the driver accelerated to pull out of Marple station, the damp morning and some minor leaf fall had reduced the coefficient of friction of the rail surface substantially. The '141' suffered considerable wheel slip. It did manage to get moving, but with an unimpressive struggle that cost over two minutes of running time.

The units received many modifications at Hunslet-Barclay, Kilmarnock, in 1988 and 1989 to improve reliability. Unit 141 113 experimentally received Cummins engines and Voith hydraulic transmissions.

Subsequent electrification of local lines out of Leeds released sufficient, newer DMUs to enable BR to sideline the '141s' by 1997. Some '141s' were sold to railways in Iran and a couple went to Holland. Three units are preserved; two are on the Weardale Railway (including 141 113 originally restored at the Llangollen Railway) and one on the Colne Valley Railway.

Class	141 'Pacer' DMUs
Details are per vehicle:	
Designed for	BR
Introduced	1984
Built by	BREL/Leyland Motors
Wheel arrgt	1-A
Layout	duo-directional with full-width cab; gangwayed within unit
Engines	1 × Leyland TL11 205bhp diesel
Transmissions	1 × Self-Change Gears mechanical gearbox
Max speed	75mph
Couplers	BSI (bar coupler within unit)
Seats	94 (2-car unit)
Heating	waste heat from engine system and oil-fired booster heater
Body length	50ft 8in
Weight in wo	26, 26.5 tons
Number built	40 vehicles
Unit numbers	141 001–20
	141 101–20 (after modification)
Vehicle numbers	55502–41.

Above: *Based on the Leyland National road bus, the narrower body of the Class 141 DMU is evident in this photograph of unit 141 003 at Marple on 30 November 1984 on the occasion of a demonstration run for local authority officials.* Author

Left: *All the Class 141 units stayed in the West Yorkshire PTE area, and soon bore that body's 'Metro Train' livery of maroon-and-cream. Refurbished No 141 116 waits at Leeds on 6 May 1989 for its departure to Knaresborough.* Author

Class 142 'Pacer' DMUs

To make better use of the BR W6 loading gauge and increase the space inside the light-weight railbus design, BR's next purchases of 'Pacer' units had wider bodies than the foregoing Class 141 type, the '142s' being 2.8 metres wide. Otherwise, the vehicles were to the same basic design but with increased seating capacity. Ninety-six Class 142 units were built, all in two-car formation. They are used widely in PTE and other urban areas. Greater Manchester employed them as part of the GMPTE network within which they received an attractive orange-and-brown livery. They were the standard units for shorter-distance routes in the conurbation and beyond. Other units in the then standard BR Provincial Services livery of pale blue worked in South Wales and in Yorkshire and the northeast, the latter in the Tyne-Wear PTE area, which later had them painted yellow. Those on Merseyside soon received a different shade of yellow, by which time West Yorkshire was using an early version of the dark red which is still its base colour today.

Some Provincial Services units, painted in a cream-and-dark brown imitation of former GWR colours, were destined for the Devon and Cornwall branches. These units experienced damage to wheelsets due to sharp curvature affecting the angle of attack of wheel treads on rail heads and causing high-pitched squealing which in turn stressed the wheel discs. At first there appeared to be no easy solution to this and the units were transferred away to join others of their brethren in the north of England.

Privatisation brought more changes of deployment for '142s', including the temporary return of some to the southwest. With their

No 142 012 rests between duties at Manchester Piccadilly on 26 April 1986. The wider body is clear when compared with the photographs on page 75. Author

Class	142 'Pacer' DMUs
Details are per vehicle:	
Designed for	BR
Introduced	1985
Built by	BREL/Leyland Motors
Wheel arrgt	1-A
Layout	duo-directional with full-width cab; gangwayed within unit
Engines	1 × Leyland TL11 205bhp diesel, replaced by Cummins LTA10-r 230bhp
Transmissions	1 × Voith T211r hydraulic torque converter; Gmeinder GM190 final drive
Max speed	75mph
Couplers	BSI (bar coupler within unit)
Seats	121* (2-car unit)
Heating	waste heat from engine system and oil-fired booster heater
Body length	51ft 0in
Weight in wo	25, 24.5 tons
Number built	192 vehicles
Unit numbers	142 001–96
Vehicle numbers	55542–641, 55701–92.

*Reduced variously in subsequent seating upgrades.

use on inter-urban routes such as Manchester to Sheffield via the Hope Valley the 'Pacers' have become the butt of criticism as being unsuitable for longer-distance runs. Current operators are Northern, Arriva Trains Wales and First Great Western, though the latter are expected to be transferred north again by the time this book is published. Three have been withdrawn due to accidents.

The Andrew Barclay-built '143' DMUs had a different frontal aspect from the earlier 'Pacers', as seen in Radyr as unit 143 601 calls with a Rhymney to Penarth service on 13 March 2003. Author

Pressure to increase the 'Pacer' fleet resulted in BR contracting Andrew Barclay and Alexander to build 25 more two-car units. These had underframes built by Barclay at Kilmarnock which were fitted with bodies by W. Alexander, the Scottish bus builder. In appearance and most details the '143' units are similar to the Class 142s, but the revised front end design clearly distinguishes them from the latter units. The body width is slightly narrower than that of the '142s', being 2.7 metres, but the seating arrangement is similar with 122 seats per two-car set.

Subsequent improvements included replacing the Leyland engines with more powerful ones from Cummins. The original bus seats have long been regarded as unsatisfactory and most 'Pacer' units, including the '143s', have been refurbished with high-backed seating.

When delivered the '143s' worked mainly in the northeast, but subsequently migrated to South Wales and the Bristol area. Arriva Trains Wales has 15 of the units and uses them in the Welsh valleys and on longer-distance services to Bristol and Taunton. First Great Western bases its smaller group at Exeter. These units work on Devon and Cornwall branch lines as well as main line stopping services. As the units are modernised, some are receiving light emitting diode (LED) clusters for their head, tail and marker lamps.

Unit 143 615 has been scrapped as a result of a fire in South Wales.

Class	143 'Pacer' DMUs
Details are per vehicle:	
Designed for	BR
Introduced	1985
Built by	Andrew Barclay/Walter Alexander
Wheel arrgt	1-A
Layout	duo-directional with full-width cab; gangwayed within unit
Engines	1 × Leyland TL11 205bhp diesel, replaced by Cummins LTA10-r 230bhp
Transmissions	1 × Voith T211r hydraulic torque converter; Gmeinder GM190 final drive
Max speed	75mph
Couplers	BSI (bar coupler within unit)
Seats	122* (2-car unit)
Heating	waste heat from engine system and oil-fired booster heater
Body length	51ft 0in
Weight in wo	25, 24.5 tons
Number built	50 vehicles
Unit numbers	143 601–625
Vehicle numbers	55642–691.

*Reduced variously in subsequent seating upgrades.

Class 144 'Pacer' DMUs

In 1986 a further 23 'Pacer' units were delivered with Alexander bodies, underframes having been subcontracted to BREL. The last 10 units were quickly extended to three-car sets by incorporating a standard-class centre car. The units are gangwayed internally. Externally they are almost identical in appearance to the '143s'. As with the '142s' and '143s', the '144s' later had their Leyland TL11 diesel engines replaced by 230bhp Cummins LTA10-r engines.

Initially liveried in the West Yorkshire PTE's dark red-and-cream colours, the '144s' have remained serving the Leeds conurbation local services throughout their lives to date. They are maintained at Neville Hill depot. Recent refurbishment has included repainting in the blue-and-purple Northern Rail colours. Despite their relatively local nature in design, Class 144 units work quite long distances on services as far as Leeds–York–Harrogate, and to Lancaster and Morecambe.

The Class 144s demonstrate the usual ride characteristics of the 'Pacer' type. Being of two-axle design, even though their suspension is a fairly modern developed design using damped flexible coil springs, their ride at speed is only good when on continuously-welded rail, that is on main lines. On jointed track with 60ft rail-lengths held together by fishplates, which is what many secondary and branch lines still have,

Class	144 'Pacer' DMUs
Details are per vehicle:	
Designed for	BR
Introduced	1986
Built by	BREL/Walter Alexander
Wheel arrgt	1-A
Layout	duo-directional with full-width cab; gangwayed within unit
Engines	1 × Leyland TL11 205bhp diesel, replaced by Cummins LTA10-r 230bhp
Transmissions	1 × Voith T211r hydraulic torque converter; Gmeinder GM190 final drive
Max speed	75mph
Couplers	BSI (bar coupler within unit)
Seats	118 (2-car unit); 190 (3-car unit)
Heating	waste heat from engine system and oil-fired booster heater
Body length	50ft 1in
Weight in wo	25, 24.5, 22.6 tons
Number built	56 vehicles
Unit numbers	144 001–13 (2-car units); 144 014–23 (3-car units)
Vehicle numbers	55801–46 (end cars), 55850–9 (intermediate cars).

The Class 144 'Pacers' looked identical to the '143s' but had been built by BREL with the same Alexander bodies. No 144 004 awaits departure from Huddersfield on 6 May 2004 with a working to Lincoln via Sheffield. The livery shows that at that time the Northern franchise was owned by Arriva, and the 'Metro Train' colours had been updated. Author

the 'Pacer' vehicles dip into the rail joints and sway from side to side in response to track alignment imperfections as well as at points and crossings. Nonetheless, at the time of writing there is no prospect of the Classes 142 to 144 being replaced by something more comfortable in which to ride.

CHAPTER 11: **BRITISH BOGIE DIESEL-HYDRAULIC MULTIPLE-UNITS**

If ever a genre of railway rolling stock was a significant leap forward using a meld of established worldwide technology, the description must include the British Rail 'Sprinter' group of units. Starting with two prototype three-car units, BREL built what appeared to be conventional DMUs but with the underfloor engine-transmission assembly based on what had proved to be successful in the Netherlands Railways' Class 3200 DMUs that had been introduced in 1983. Under each car a Cummins diesel engine was coupled to a Voith hydraulic torque converter transmission which switched to direct drive at a specified speed. Both pieces of traction equipment were of robust design and construction. They drove all four wheels on one bogie through cardan shafts and gears.

The Class 150 'Sprinter' prototypes used bodies based on those of the Classes 317 and 455 EMUs but with full-width cabs and gangwayed only within the units. Bogies were based on BREL's highly successful BX series with damped air-bag secondary suspension which gave an excellent ride at all speeds. Maximum speed was set at 75mph. The vehicle floor included a solid steel plate over the engine-transmission area. This would prevent any upward incursion of unwanted mechanical parts into the vehicle in the unlikely event of an engine or cardan shaft breaking up.

Each vehicle had two batteries, one for starting the engine and a separate one for auxiliaries such as lighting and traction control. Internally the vehicles had composition floor surfaces, plastic wall linings and 3 + 2 outer suburban seating with two toilets per three-car set. In short, little of the engineering was actually innovative, but all was either proven elsewhere or in other BR stock, or was introduced as a result of experience with first-generation DMUs. The result was a step-change in advance of reliability and availability. The Class 150 fleet performed extremely reliably.

Metro-Cammell had introduced in parallel its Class 151 prototype (page 122), which was not pursued. However, the company was given the opportunity three years later to build the Class 156 two-car units for longer-distance inter-urban use. The author recalls his first impressions of these units when walking into one of the first off the production line. The immediately noticeable differences were the passenger entrance doors being at the saloon ends, the lower-density seating, and the use of carpets in all standard-class saloons, a first on BR DMUs other than the Pullman units. The '156s' proved popular, and are indeed even today quite acceptable on most of their routes.

The bus builder Leyland produced from 1987 the Class 155 units that were a parallel development for the same market as the '156s'. With the exception of the group of '155s' that were funded by West Yorkshire PTE, the rest of the class were subsequently converted to single-vehicle railcars

with a cab at each end (page 83), intended both for low-traffic-volume routes and for strengthening other DMUs.

In 1989 BREL developed the 'Super-Sprinter' principle with the '158' and '159' classes, these in effect being main line trains, albeit in two- or three-car formations. These were quieter units in which to ride due mainly to their non-opening windows and air-conditioning. The group became the front-line BR DMU for longer-distance services until the advent of newer types in the 1990s and after privatisation.

Having developed the specifications for the Networker EMUs it was logical for BR to require a DMU version, which emerged as the Classes 165 and 166. Known as 'Networker Turbos', these made use of the wider loading gauge inherited from the Brunel era of the Great Western Railway with maximum body width set at 2.81 metres. They are used on the Chiltern lines out of London Marylebone as well as on Paddington commuter services.

Privatisation brought innovation in some train operators' services, none more than Chiltern which aimed at taking a share of the lucrative Birmingham–London market. The Class 168 units were air-conditioned sets, three- and four-car units, with a 100mph top speed. The logical development from this design was the Class 170 and its derivatives which became BREL's successors' (Adtranz and Bombardier) standard vehicle for most future multiple-unit applications, known generally as 'Turbostars' (DMUs) and 'Electrostars' (EMUs).

Alstom entered the modern DMU market with its 'Coradia' and 'Adelante' units, the former Class 175s for inter-urban use and the latter Class 180s for 125mph main line services to supplement HSTs. The '175s' are based at the Alstom-run depot at Chester for scheduled maintenance and work in the area Manchester–Crewe–North and South Wales. The Class 180 has to date had a chequered career, being deemed unreliable by First Great Western who passed them over for more HSTs. They have since found work with operators on the east coast main line serving destinations off the electrified routes.

The latest development of the type has come from Siemens which had great success with its 'Desiro' EMUs and developed a DMU version which is used by the Trans-Pennine Express operating franchise. This is a heavyweight, powerful design with 100mph operating speed and air-conditioning.

Future new DMU building at the time of writing looks unlikely for some years as we enter a period of fiscal retrenchment. A policy to build 200 new DMU vehicles was abandoned in 2010, with no follow-up orders in sight.

The first prototype Class 150 unit served its purpose as a demonstrator, seen at Derby on 3 September 1984, and was later absorbed as a standard member of the class. Author

Class	150 'Sprinter' DMUs
Details are per vehicle:	
Designed for	BR
Introduced	1984
Built by	BREL York
Wheel arrgt	2-B
Layout	duo-directional with full-width cab (150/0 and 150/1); gangwayed outer ends and half-width cab (150/2); all gangwayed within unit
Engines	1 × Cummins NT855R5 285bhp diesel
Transmissions	1 × Voith T211r hydraulic torque converter; Gmeinder GM190 final drive
Max speed	75mph*
Couplers	BSI (bar coupler within unit)
Seats	70 to 76
Heating	waste heat from engine system and oil-fired booster heater
Body length	67ft 7in
Weight in wo	34.9 to 38.45 tonnes
Number built	276 vehicles
Unit numbers	150 001–19, 22; 150 101, 102, 120, 121, 123–150; 150 201–285**
Vehicle numbers	55200–1, 55300–1, 55400–1, 52101–50, 52201–85, 57101–50, 57201–85.

* 154 002 had 90mph maximum for short period from 1986.
** Less 150/2s (202, 204, 206, 209, 210, 212, 214, 216, 220, 226) disbanded to make up 3-car '150/0' units.

Two prototype Class 150 DMU three-car sets were put in service in 1984 and were sufficiently promising for the first production batch of 50 units to be ordered and delivered by BREL York Works for BR's Provincial Services sector from 1985. The production units were originally formed as two-car sets. These '150s' have full-width cabs and are gangwayed within the units, the two-car sets being classified '150/1'. From 1986 a further 85 two-car units were built, this time with gangways at the outer ends as well as within the units. These are classified '150/2'.

As an experiment in 1986, to develop the potential for a 90mph express DMU (see class 158 on page 83), 150 002 was modified with a higher drive gear ratio. Temporarily renumbered 154 002, it proved the practical ability of the bogies to run smoothly at the higher speed, but demonstrated a slower rate of acceleration from stops. The '154' later reverted to its original gear ratio and was reclassified '150'.

In operation the '150s' in all their varieties reach high reliability and availability when compared with the first-generation DMUs which they replaced. They are used on all former BR regions except the SR, though the Leeds-based ones have been replaced by other types and have moved to the northwest. Their 1/3rd 2/3rd door layout, with double-leaf sliding doors, fits them to suburban or inter-urban roles and they are common on main line stopping services.

In the West Midlands about 20 '150' units have been strengthened by inserting one Class 150/2 vehicle (from a disbanded unit) in the middle, producing a three-car unit gangwayed internally but still with non-gangwayed ends. These are now Class 150/0. These, as well as several

'150/1s', are used on Birmingham area suburban workings, mainly from Snow Hill and Moor Street stations. The main depots for maintenance of '150s' are Newton Heath in Manchester, Tyseley in Birmingham, Cardiff Canton and Plymouth Laira. A small number of two-car units was based at Willesden for London area services, but these have been displaced by Class 172 units.

Above left: *'Sprinter' unit 150 133 in Regional Railways livery calls at Deansgate with a Buxton to Blackpool North service in 1992.* Author

Below left: *The temporary '154' experiment enabled 154 002 to run at 90mph, but with slower acceleration. The unit passes Stenson Junction on 27 August 1991.* Peter Swift

Below: *The '150/2' series were gangwayed throughout giving more operational flexibility. On 13 June 1987, No 150 253 awaits departure from Blaenau Ffestiniog for Llandudno.* Author

Designed for longer-distance services, the Class 156 two-car units began to appear from Metro-Cammell's Washwood Heath factory in Birmingham in 1987. Gangwayed throughout, the '156s' set new standards for comfort in DMUs with higher-backed seats and carpeted floors in the saloons. They were deployed by the Provincial Services, later Regional Railways, sector of BR which used them in the northeast, the north, East Anglia, the Midlands and Scotland.

The '156s' have the same power-transmission set-up as the '150s', and can multiple with them as well as with all other 'Sprinter' and 'Pacer' variants. They have steel bodies on integral underframes, and the maximum speed is a modest 75mph. Passenger access doors are single-leaf sliding doors recessed into the bodyside at the vehicle ends.

Post-privatisation, the '156s' are the staple units on scenic routes such as the Leeds–Carlisle line and the Scottish routes to the north and the isles. Those on the West Highland and routes to the north are fitted for radio token block working. Current operators include Northern, East Midlands Trains, London Midland, National Express Anglia and ScotRail together with Strathclyde Partnership for Transport. As one of the most successful of the second-generation DMU types, the '156s' are maintained at Glasgow Corkerhill, Heaton (Newcastle-on Tyne), Newton Heath (Manchester), Neville Hill (Leeds), Norwich Crown Point and Tyseley (Birmingham).

As with all second-generation DMUs, changes in train operator have led to several upgrades of the interior as well as livery changes. Unlike the '150s', the '156s' have always had medium-density seating in a 2 + 2 layout. They are not air-conditioned, and the use of hopper windows has its disadvantages, particularly on a hot day when open windows reflect external noise back into the saloon, a situation they share with the lower-numbered 'Sprinter' series units.

Class	156 'Super Sprinter' DMUs
Details are per vehicle:	
Designed for	BR
Introduced	1987
Built by	Metro-Cammell
Wheel arrgt	2-B
Layout	duo-directional with half-width cab; gangwayed throughout
Engines	1 × Cummins NT855R5 285bhp diesel
Transmissions	1 × Voith T211r hydraulic torque converter; Gmeinder GM190 final drive
Max speed	75mph
Couplers	BSI (bar coupler within unit)
Seats	68 to 78
Heating	waste heat from engine system and oil-fired booster heater
Body length	75ft 7in
Weight in wo	37.9, 38.6 tonnes
Number built	228 vehicles
Unit numbers	156 401–514
Vehicle numbers	52401–514, 57401–514.

Passing Attenborough near Nottingham en route for Derby is unit 156 410. The 'Super-Sprinters' had 23-metre-long bodies and carpets in all saloons. The '156s' were Metro-Cammell products. Author

Class 155 'Super Sprinter' DMUs

Class	155 'Super Sprinter' DMUs
Details are per vehicle:	
Designed for	BR
Introduced	1987
Built by	Leyland Motors, Workington
Wheel arrgt	2-B
Layout	duo-directional with half-width cab; gangwayed throughout
Engines	1 × Cummins NT855R5 285bhp diesel
Transmissions	1 × Voith T211r hydraulic torque converter; Gmeinder GM190 final drive
Max speed	75mph
Couplers	BSI (bar coupler within unit)
Seats	76, 80
Heating	waste heat from engine system and oil-fired booster heater
Body length	76ft 2in
Weight in wo	39, 38.6 tonnes
Number built	84 vehicles
Unit numbers	155 301–35,* 155 341–7
Vehicle numbers	52301–35,* 52341–7, 57301–35,* 57341–47

* Rebuilt 1991–2 as two-cab single railcars, Class 153.

In parallel with the '156s', in 1987 Leyland Motors at Workington began production of 42 two-car 'Super Sprinters' for the same duty range. These had similarities in body construction with the 'Pacers', having light-weight riveted steel body panels. The use of standard bus components forced the cars to have windows that were much shorter than usual on inter-urban railway carriages, resulting in many more being needed in the length of a 23-metre long vehicle. An innovation for British DMUs was the use of swing-plug doors in place of the more usual sliding doors. The last seven units were funded and owned by West Yorkshire Passenger Transport Executive. While the earlier units were delivered in BR's Regional Railways livery of two-tone grey with blue bands, the PTE units began life in WYPTE red. All have since received other liveries as tastes and ownerships change.

For a time, the '155s' proved to be unreliable. They were mostly based at Cardiff for South Wales and longer-distance services. Doors opening in traffic caused serious worry about passenger safety, and the units were withdrawn temporarily for modifications to be carried out, particularly to make door operation more reliable. However, 1991 saw a major development with 35 Class 155 units being rebuilt as single car double-cab vehicles. These are described on page 83. The seven WYPTE-owned '155' units were not so rebuilt and remain in service as two-car sets. These work mainly around Leeds on services to York via Harrogate, and Leeds to Manchester Victoria over the Calder Valley line. Based at Neville Hill for maintenance, they have settled in to a satisfactory reliability level.

The short life of the first 35 two-car units was unique in the annals of British second-generation DMUs. All were originally in the two-tone blue Regional Railways livery of the day. The seven PTE units are now in the standard livery of Northern, the train operator within whose area they work.

Above: *Emerging from Salisbury tunnel on 17 September 1991 while on a Portsmouth Harbour to Cardiff service is Leyland-built unit 155 329. Most of these sets were subsequently split up and rebuilt to form the Class 153 single cars. Author*

Below: *The '155s' that were funded by West Yorkshire PTE remain as twin sets. No 155 346 was way outside the WYPTE area when photographed at Blackpool North in 1991. Author*

Converted from a '155' vehicle by fitting a small cab (far end in this picture), BR produced some useful single diesel railcars. No 153 302 at Derby on 2 July 2010 is in East Midlands Trains livery and will soon set off for Crewe. Author

In the earlier years of British Railways it seemed that no railway line could survive long when it needed only one carriage on its passenger trains. Thus it came as a surprise to many when BR's Regional Railways sector decided that it needed a significant number of single DMU vehicles. Thirty-five of the relatively unloved Class 155 two-car units were split up and each car rebuilt at one end to provide an additional driving cab, albeit a somewhat shorter one than usual. This was achieved by fitting the new cab between the passenger access doorway vestibule and the front of the vehicle; in view of the less roomy cab that would result, drivers' unions were consulted before this was done.

The 70 vehicles of Class 153 cover some of the less remunerative, more heavily supported, services more economically than would two-car units. The '153s' are also used to strengthen other trains where two-car trains are not enough but a four-car would be excessive. Since privatisation they have been scattered between train operators and work in the north of England, East Anglia, the Midlands, Wales and the West Country.

Interestingly, one can find refurbished East Midlands Trains '153s' on the Derby to Crewe line. This was previously served by two-car DMUs, usually '156s', working an hourly Nottingham–Manchester Airport service. When the route was cut back to terminate at Crewe, some patronage dropped off, and since then the Nottingham end has been cut back to Derby and a single car each hour is generally sufficient.

Class	153 single DMUs
Details are per vehicle:	
Designed for	BR
Introduced	1991*
Rebuilt by	Hunslet-Barclay, Kilmarnock*
Wheel arrgt	2-B
Layout	duo-directional with two half-width cabs; gangwayed throughout
Engines	1 × Cummins NT855R5 285bhp diesel
Transmissions	1 × Voith T211r hydraulic torque converter; Gmeinder GM190 final drive
Max speed	75mph
Couplers	BSI (bar coupler within unit)
Seats	69, 72
Heating	waste heat from engine system and oil-fired booster heater
Body length	76ft 2in
Weight in wo	41.2 tonnes
Number rebuilt	70 vehicles*
Unit numbers	153 301–35, 153 351–85
Original veh Nos	52301–35, 57301–35
1992 vehicle Nos	52301–35, 57351–85

* Originally built 1987-8 by Leyland Motors as Class 155 two-car DMUs.

Refurbishment of these units has improved the interiors. Some further work is in progress on units working in scenic areas such as on the Central Wales Line; this is to raise the level of seating so that passengers have a better view through the windows. Nonetheless, the lack of air-conditioning and the need to open windows for ventilation makes a journey in one of these cars quite noisy.

Class 158 DMUs

Whereas previous DMUs built by BREL were steel bodied, the need to add air-conditioning gave impetus for designers to find ways of keeping down the weight of the Class 158 express DMUs, including the use of welded aluminium for the vehicle bodies. These were 23 metre-long, 2.7 metre-wide vehicles built as two-car sets for higher-speed services on secondary main lines. With a pair of folding swing-plug doors at each end of the vehicle, passenger access and egress is necessarily slower than from the earlier '150' series units with their wider sliding doors along the bodysides. Well insulated and with a top speed of 90mph, the '158s' ride smoothly and are among the better DMUs in the British national fleet. Thus it comes as no surprise that they are the biggest class numerically of all BR-specified second-generation DMUs.

Three engine types are in use on '158s', namely a Cummins 350bhp engine, a later version of the same engine but rated at 400bhp, and a Perkins engine of 350bhp. All use the standard Voith hydraulic transmission. As with all second-generation DMUs, the '158s' have air-operated brakes, but not with tread brake blocks as on the earlier units; the '158s', by dint of their higher operating speed, need a higher performance brake system and have disc brakes. During autumn when leaves fall on the railway, clasp brake blocks are able to scrape debris off the wheel treads but disc brakes, operating on cheek discs, do not do this. Mulch builds up on the wheel treads and causes poor adhesion. The units have since been fitted with scrubbing blocks.

Some sets are now operating as three-car units on Northern services and on South West Trains where three units are supplementing that company's Class 159 fleet (see page 85).

In 1991 BREL exported 12 three-car sets built for the metre gauge railways of Thailand. These work express trains out of Bangkok. Originally delivered in the same livery as Regional Railways, they are being overhauled and repainted in 2011.

Class	158 DMUs
Details are per vehicle:	
Designed for	BR
Introduced	1989
Built by	BREL Derby
Wheel arrgt	2-B
Layout	duo-directional with half-width cab; gangwayed throughout
Engines	1 × Cummins NT855R 350bhp diesel (158 701–814); 1 × Perkins 2006-TWH 350bhp (158 815–62); 1 × Cummins NTA855R 400bhp (158 863–72)
Transmissions	1 × Voith T211r hydraulic torque converter; Gmeinder GM190 final drive
Max speed	90mph
Couplers	BSI (bar coupler within unit)
Seats	64 to 70
Heating	air-conditioned
Body length	76ft 2in
Weight in wo	38.5 tonnes
Number built	340 vehicles*
Unit numbers	158 701–872, 158 901–910**
Vehicle numbers	52701–872, 52901–10,* 57701–57872, 57901–10,* 58701–17***

*   Excludes eight 3-car units (Nos 158 800–1, 3–5, 7, 9, 11) converted during 2006/7 to Class 159/1 (page 84).
** Ten '158' 2-car sets built for West Yorkshire PTE.
*** Non-driving intermediate power cars for 3-car sets.

The '158' class were the first UK DMUs to be fully air-conditioned. No 158 745 awaits departure from Bristol Temple Meads on 13 April 2002 with a service for Portsmouth Harbour. Author

Built at the end of the Class 158 order, and before entering traffic, the 22 three-car units that became Class 159 were upgraded by Rosyth Dockyard for South West Trains' long-distance services between London Waterloo, Salisbury and Exeter. As before, their construction employed welded aluminium bodyshells, 400bhp Cummins engines and hydraulic transmissions, gangways throughout and the ability to multiple with all variants of the '14X' and '15X' series DMUs. The upgrade included more suitable, lower-density seating for long-distance journeys. Indeed their internal environment is among the best of the BR-designed DMU fleet. Still using the standard BR-designed air-sprung bolsterless bogies and being well insulated, the ride is both smooth and reasonably quiet.

South West Trains (SWT), managed by the Stagecoach franchise, elected to start as they meant to go on, with a brand new maintenance depot at Salisbury in the middle of the route. This investment, including the training of newly-recruited maintenance personnel in the methods to be used, has paid off. The '159s' are consistently among the best-performing ex-BR DMUs in terms of reliability and availability.

The '159s' work the regular interval services from London Waterloo to Salisbury and Exeter, peak hour trains usually being made up of three three-car units in multiple. Most other services east of Salisbury are six cars, whereas those heading west to Exeter are often reduced to a single three-car unit. For several years services were extended to Plymouth. At the time of writing the Exeter–Plymouth stopping trains are covered by First Great Western, the displaced '159' units helping to cope with traffic growth on SWT. Class 159 diagrams have also seen the units work services to Southampton and Portsmouth.

Further traffic growth gave rise to the need for more DMUs on the Salisbury and Exeter main line. Eight Class 158 units were transferred to SWT in 2006/7. These have been subsumed into Class 159 during heavy overhaul and refurbishment and have become Class 159/1.

Class	159 DMUs
Details are per vehicle:	
Designed for	BR
Introduced	1992
Built by	BREL Derby
Wheel arrgt	2-B
Layout	duo-directional with half-width cab; gangwayed throughout
Engines	1 × Cummins NTA855R3 400bhp (158 863–72)
Transmissions	1 × Voith T211r hydraulic torque converter; Gmeinder GM190 final drive
Max speed	90mph
Couplers	BSI (bar coupler within unit)
Seats	52, 70, 72
Heating	air-conditioned
Body length	76ft 2in
Weight in wo	38.5 tonnes
Number built	90 vehicles*
Unit numbers	159 001–22, 159 101–108
Vehicle numbers	52873–94, 57873–94, 58718–39; 52800–1, 3–5, 7, 9, 11, 57800–1, 3–5, 7, 9, 11, 58701, 3–5, 7, 9, 11, 17.

* Includes eight 3-car Class 159/1 units converted during 2006/7 from Class 158 (page 83).

For South West Trains services to Salisbury and Exeter the operator wanted DMUs like the '158s' but to a higher internal specification. The resultant Class 159s have an excellent reputation for reliability due to the attention they receive at the dedicated new depot at Salisbury. Unit 159 009 leads two others in a nine-car formation on an Up peak working passing Winchfield on 15 July 2010. Author

Class 165 'Networker Turbo' DMUs

The project to replace first-generation BR DMUs from the suburban lines radiating out of the Paddington and Marylebone terminals in London led to a more innovative approach to carriage design. At that time BR was developing the 'Networker' EMU specification and it was logical to incorporate new suburban DMUs in the same group. Indeed, the DMUs appeared first, in 1990. The BR business responsible was Network SouthEast, with its Thames & Chiltern service group receiving the allocation, which was assigned to Reading for maintenance. The first units were 28 two-car units, followed by 11 three-car sets, all for the Marylebone line services. Because the Great Western and Great Central Railways had generous loading gauges, the '165s' were able to have 23-metre-long bodies with a width of 2.81 metres. Use on other parts of the BR system would thereafter need special checks on clearances before permission could be given. The cars have a typical suburban layout with double swing-plug doors at 1/3rd and 2/3rd positions on the bodysides. They are gangwayed within the units and have full-width cabs. These units were followed in 1992 by 17 three-car units for the Paddington line services to Reading and beyond, and another 20 two-car units. While the Chiltern sets are limited to 75mph, the Paddington area sets have a 90mph top speed.

After privatisation the '165' fleets were split up, the Chiltern Line units (Class 165/0) soon being transferred to a purpose-built new maintenance depot at Aylesbury. A significant refurbishing from 2003 fitted air-conditioning and upgraded seating to these units, the first-class areas being reduced to standard class in most sets, but to a higher standard of comfort.

The First Great Western units (now known as Class 165/1) have also been internally refreshed, but these retain their small first-class compartments at one end. These units remain without air-conditioning.

Class	165 'Networker Turbo' DMUs
Details are per vehicle:	
Designed for	BR
Introduced	1990
Built by	BREL York
Wheel arrgt	2-B
Layout	duo-directional with full-width cab; gangwayed within units
Engines	1 × Perkins 2006-TWH 350bhp diesel
Transmissions	1 × Voith T211r hydraulic torque converter; Gmeinder GM190 final drive
Max speed	75mph, 90mph*
Couplers	BSI (bar coupler within unit)
Seats	89, 94, 106; 82, 92, 98, 106*
Heating	waste heat from engine system and oil-fired booster heater**
Body length	77ft 1in
Weight in wo	37, 38 tonnes**
Number built	180 vehicles
Unit numbers	165 001–39, 165 101–137*
Vehicle numbers	58801–78, 58879–98,* 58916–69,* 55404–14, 55415–31*.

*   Class 165/1.
** Class 165/0 were fitted with trip-cocks for working on joint Met/GCR line; fitted with air-conditioning from 2003, weight increased to 37, 39.4 and 40.1 tonnes.

Wider bodies were used in BREL's next DMU design, the Class 165s for the Thames & Chiltern section of Network SouthEast. No 165 117 approaches Reading on a service from London Paddington on 13 December 1992. Author

The express version of the '165' was the Class 166 design. The Thames Trains livery on 166 214 has been rebranded by FirstGroup, but it is yet to receive the full dark blue livery. The train is calling at Reading en route for Newbury on 18 June 2004. Author

For the London Paddington to Oxford fast commuter trains, the BR sector Network SouthEast (NSE) ordered a further 21 three-car sets based on the Class 165 (page 86) but with air-conditioning from new and a maximum speed of 90mph. They have a first-class compartment at each end of the unit, and two toilet compartments in each unit. In other respects the units were identical to the two versions of '165s'. Although fitted with standard BSI Tightlock automatic couplings at the outer ends, they could only multiple with each other and with Class 165 units. Control circuits did not match those on the earlier BR second-generation DMUs with similar couplings. This was not a serious operating restraint as their duties rarely took them into areas where 'Sprinter'-type DMUs worked, and the Thames & Chiltern area of NSE at that time had no other classes of modern DMU in its fleet.

Although the units were similar in carriage design to the 'Networker' EMUs, there was one significant feature of the latter that was not fitted to the '165' and '166' DMUs, namely the override buffers at the end of vehicles. This only became a safety requirement in 1991, and these DMUs escaped the requirement in the interests of standardisation between the two classes of these unique fleets.

When built, the units wore the colourful blue-red-and-white livery of Network SouthEast. After privatisation they were repainted in the appropriate

Class	166 'Networker Express' DMUs
Details are per vehicle:	
Designed for	BR
Introduced	1990
Built by	ABB York
Wheel arrgt	2-B
Layout	duo-directional with full-width cab; gangwayed within units
Engines	1 × Perkins 2006-TWH 350bhp diesel
Transmissions	1 × Voith T211r hydraulic torque converter; Gmeinder GM190 final drive
Max speed	90mph
Couplers	BSI (bar coupler within unit)
Seats	88, 95, 96
Heating	air-conditioned
Body length	77ft 1in
Weight in wo	39.6, 38 tonnes
Number built	63 vehicles
Unit numbers	166 201–21
Vehicle numbers	58101–42, 58601–21.

liveries of Chiltern Rail or Thames Trains. The latter's last livery for these trains was blue-and-off white with bright green splashes across the doors. This gave way to all-over dark blue with wavy lines when FirstGroup, which had taken over and combined the Thames and Great Western franchises, settled on its definitive livery.

Class 168 'Clubman' DMUs

Initially to probe the market, Chiltern Rail obtained five three-car express DMUs from Adtranz in Derby (Adtranz had taken over ABB's rolling stock interests which had previously purchased BREL) to work between London Marylebone and Birmingham Snow Hill. The strategy was to provide a lower-fare, good quality travel experience between Birmingham and London when compared with the more expensive, faster west coast main line. The units were designed for a maximum speed of 100mph and were fully air-conditioned. To achieve the higher maximum speed, more powerful engines were sourced from the German company MTU. These were the first DMUs to be delivered to the railway network after privatisation.

As built, the units included a first-class section but, in a bid to increase capacity, this was replaced by standard class when the units were subsequently refurbished to a higher general internal quality. The body design follows the 23 metre length of most inter-urban DMUs with the width limited to 2.7 metres to give universal route availability. After four years the units were extended to four-car sets by taking intermediate power cars from a second order of four-car units, known as Class 168/1.

Further 'Clubman' units were delivered by Adtranz and its successor Bombardier between 2000 and 2006, the latter year being when an additional batch of intermediate power cars was built to strengthen some three-car sets to four vehicles. These later units, Classes 168/1 and 168/2, are of the same basic design as the Class 170 'Turbostar' units described on page 89; they are distinguishable from the earliest '168s' by their different front end design. In their current formations, there are 10 four-car units and nine three-car sets within the 'Clubman' brand.

Right: Chiltern Railways' unit No 168 003 passes Tyseley on 25 August 2006 while working the 19.12 from Birmingham Snow Hill to London Marylebone. Peter Swift

Below: The later varieties of the Chiltern Railways '168s' are of the 'Turbostar' family. Here is 168 110 approaching Princes Risborough on 23 October 2008, with the 10.20 from London Marylebone to Birmingham Snow Hill. Brian Morrison

Below right: The Class 168/2s are externally very similar to the '168/1' units but the head and tail lamp clusters have been modified on the later units. On 5 June 2008, No 168 214 calls at Banbury on a southbound working. Ian Copplestone

Class	168 'Clubman' DMUs
Details are per vehicle:	
Designed for	BR/Chiltern Railways
Introduced	1997
Built by	Adtranz/Bombardier Derby
Wheel arrgt	2-B
Layout	duo-directional with full-width cab; gangwayed within units
Engines	1 × MTU 6R183TD13H 422bhp diesel
Transmissions	1 × Voith T211rzze hydraulic torque converter; ZF reversing final drive
Max speed	100mph
Couplers	BSI (bar coupler within unit)
Seats	60 to 77
Heating	air-conditioned
Body length	77ft 6in
Weight in wo	40.5 to 45.5 tonnes
Number built	15 (168/0), 31 (168/1),* 21 (168/2) vehicles, total 67
Unit numbers	168 001–5, 106–13, 214–9
Vehicle numbers	58151–69, 58251–69, 58365–7, 58451–69,** 58651–5, 58756–7.

* Includes five intermediate cars for 168/0 units.
** Vehicles 58451–5 and 58461–3 previously carried numbers 58656–63.

Alstom was producing several variations of its 'Coradia' range of multiple-units on the European continent when it made a bid for two-car and three-car DMUs for First North Western services between Manchester and Wales. Like other overseas suppliers that have bid for UK train contracts, Alstom was somehow discouraged from offering a UK version of its well-established 'Coradia' articulated units, and opted for a new design of double-bogie vehicle laid out in the traditional British way. Preliminary testing was done on the Severn Valley Railway and then on the Old Dalby test track south of Nottingham. As always happens when new designs are produced in quantity without previously being tried and tested, the first units suffered many teething troubles before being ready enough for regular service.

This was unfortunate, because in reality the Class 175 is a conventional two- or three-car air-conditioned DMU with little conceptual originality to distinguish it from other suppliers' offerings such as the 'Turbostars'. Aimed at the inter-urban market, the '175' has single-leaf swing-plug passenger access doors at the body ends and a standard seat layout of 2 + 2 with the high-backed seating that has become recommended for safety reasons. With a top speed of 100mph, aided by a 450bhp Cummins engine under each car, the '175s' are express units with a good rate of acceleration.

The North Western franchise was later joined up with Northern Spirit to form the new Northern franchise, but with Trans-Pennine Express (TPE) split off as a separate franchise. Some '175s' went to TPE, but all were later allocated to Arriva Trains Wales. Through all these changes, the 11 two-car

Class	175 'Coradia' DMUs
Details are per vehicle:	
Designed for	First North Western
Introduced	1999
Built by	Alstom, Washwood Heath
Wheel arrgt	2-B
Layout	duo-directional with full-width cab; gangwayed within units
Engines	1 × Cummins N14 450bhp diesel
Transmissions	1 × Voith T211rzze hydraulic torque converter; ZF reversing final drive; hydrodynamic retarder
Max speed	100mph
Couplers	Scharfenberg (bar coupler within unit)
Seats	54, 64, 68
Heating	air-conditioned
Body length	77ft 9in, 75ft 7in
Weight in wo	50.7, 47.5 tonnes
Number built	70 vehicles
Unit numbers	175 001–11, 175 101–16
Vehicle numbers	50701–11, 79701–11; 50751–66, 56751–66, 79751–66.

and 16 three-car units continued to be maintained at Alstom's purpose-built depot at Chester. In recent years, product support there has improved, and the 'Coradias' are providing successful services for their franchisee.

Left: *The Alstom '175' class is part of the company's 'Coradia' brand. Based at Chester depot, the units work fast services linking English cities with North and South Wales. 175 001 was being tested on the Severn Valley Railway at Kidderminster on 9 October 1999.* Author

Below: *In Arriva Trains Wales livery, No 175 002 approaches Abergavenny on 13 April 2010. These units are air-conditioned and have long saloons with end doors.* Author

Class 180 'Adelante' DMUs

There was considerable excitement in the year 2000 at the introduction of two quite different types of DMU intended to extend the number of high speed trains in the UK that were capable of 125mph. Alstom followed the '175s' with another variant of the 'Coradia' family, though First Great Western (FGW) opted to call them 'Adelante'. The five-car Class 180 is a sleek-looking train indeed. Inside the seating is comfortable, the layout reasonably spacious, the ride acceptable and the running quiet apart from the faint underfloor drumming of the big diesel engine. This was a Cummins engine designed to produce 750bhp, and there was one under each car, so the '180' was no mean machine when considering performance on the road.

FGW began by using them on the Bristol, Exeter and Hereford lines. Troublesome reliability, however, caused the 'Adelantes' to be relegated more to the marginal routes such as to Worcester and to Oxford outer suburban services. FGW had decided by 2007 that it was going to lease more of the venerable HSTs for its inter-city services and that it would take the '180s' off lease.

They did not spend long in store. Hull Trains decided to take the opportunity to lease two of these trains to cover for a damaged four-car Class 222 'Pioneer' unit. The company later received four '180s' and sent its '222s' over to East Midlands Trains (page 102). Meanwhile the other east coast main line open access operator Grand Central leased five units to join its HST fleet, particularly for services from London King's Cross to Bradford. Three more are temporarily in the hands of Northern Rail for peak services across the Pennines though leased to East Coast; two other East Coast sets are in store at the time of writing.

Class	180 'Adelante' DMUs
Details are per vehicle:	
Designed for	First Great Western
Introduced	2000
Built by	Alstom, Washwood Heath
Wheel arrgt	2-B
Layout	duo-directional with full-width, streamlined cab; gangwayed within units
Engines	1 × Cummins QSK19 750bhp diesel
Transmissions	1 × Voith T312BRE hydraulic torque converter; ZF reversing final drive; hydrodynamic retarder
Max speed	125mph
Couplers	Scharfenberg (bar coupler within unit)
Seats	33, 72, 64
Heating	air-conditioned
Body length	77ft 9in, 75ft 7in
Weight in wo	49.5 to 51.7 tonnes
Number built	70 vehicles
Unit numbers	180 101–14
Vehicle numbers	50901–14, 54901–14, 55901–14, 56901–14, 59901–14.

These smaller operators have managed to tame the '180s'' unreliability sufficiently by (in the words of one maintenance engineer) giving them sufficient 'tender loving care' to keep them in good technical condition.

Above: *The other DMU 'Coradia' design that emerged for the privatised railway was the Class 180. First Great Western gave the class the name 'Adelante'. This one was at Bristol Temple Meads on 13 March 2003. The class was later taken off lease due to perceived unreliability.* Author

Right: *Open access operators, in particular Grand Central, made use of the '180s' on services from London King's Cross to Hull and West Yorkshire. At Bradford Interchange on 12 June 2010, unit 180 114 is being prepared for departure to London.* Author

The German company of Siemens, when bidding for a contract to supply its first DMUs to the UK market, based the design on its successful Class 450 'Desiro UK' outer-suburban EMUs that were in use in the south of England. Traction is a 750bhp Cummins engine under each car driving through a Voith hydraulic transmission. For trains with a maximum speed of 100mph, this apparently high power/weight ratio of 13.8bhp/tonne is to enable the units to accelerate quickly, but more importantly to maintain line speeds up the steep gradients on the routes between West Yorkshire and Lancashire through the Pennine hills. Nonetheless, these units are heavier than most UK DMUs.

The carriage bodies are similar to the EMUs on which they are based except that the '185s' have full-width cabs and are only gangwayed between vehicles within a set. Seating is suitable for inter-urban work and the trains offer a more pleasant travel experience than do many current UK DMUs. However, in addition to working across the Pennines, these units currently are also working the former InterCity service between Manchester and Glasgow, rather a long journey time to be subject to the underfloor engine noise of a DMU. The '185s' are maintained at new depots at York and Manchester.

The franchisee, Trans-Pennine Express (TPE), has taken recent steps to reduce fuel consumption on these trains. When not needing the highest level of power to climb gradients or make up time, drivers can initiate an economy mode in which one or other of the three engines in the unit are shut down, the remaining 1,500bhp being more than adequate to maintain normal timings on more easily-graded sections with a three-car train.

TPE would like to extend capacity on its more overcrowded services by obtaining more Class 185 units, or by extending some to four cars. The

Class	185 'Desiro' DMUs
Details are per vehicle:	
Designed for	First Trans-Pennine
Introduced	2005
Built by	Siemens, Uerdingen, Germany
Wheel arrgt	2-B
Layout	duo-directional with full-width cab; gangwayed within units
Engines	1 × Cummins QSK19 750bhp diesel
Transmissions	1 × Voith T312BRE hydraulic torque converter; ZF reversing final drive; hydrodynamic retarder
Max speed	100mph
Couplers	Dellner (bar coupler within unit)
Seats	33, 72, 64
Heating	air-conditioned
Body length	77ft 11in
Weight in wo	52.7 to 55.4 tonnes
Number built	153 vehicles
Unit numbers	185 101–51
Vehicle numbers	51101–51, 53101–51, 54101–51.

government cancellation in 2010 of the programme to acquire 200 new DMU vehicles for the national network has currently prevented that from happening.

First Trans-Pennine Express operates these Class 185 units which are a DMU version of the Siemens 'Desiro' outer-suburban EMU. This one is approaching York on test on 14 July 2006. Author

IÉ Class 2600 Tokyu railcars

Many years after the first-generation diesel railcars on CIÉ had been withdrawn, in 1993 Irish Rail took delivery of the first of 17 single-ended diesel railcars from the Tokyu Car Company of Japan. These were similar in layout to the British Rail Class 150/2 DMUs (page 80). Gangwayed inside and out of sets, they had access doors at the 1/3rd and 2/3rd positions. They used a Cummins 350bhp diesel engine under each car driving a Japanese hydraulic torque converter. Shafts took the drive through a gearbox on each axle of the outer bogie to the wheelsets. The vehicles are air-braked with two discs per axle.

The railcars operate in two-car units. The odd vehicle was originally used as a maintenance spare car, then ran coupled to a '2700' series railcar to form an additional unit. The original livery was an up-market version of the then standard gold, black-and-white that had been used on locomotives and hauled stock. This was changed from 2003 into a lime green-based livery with white and dark blue decoration.

Class	IÉ 2600 railcars
Details are per vehicle:	
Designed for	Iarnród Éireann
Introduced	1993
Built by	Tokyu Car Co, Japan
Wheel arrgt	B-2
Layout	duo-directional with half-width, cab; gangwayed throughout
Engine	1 × Cummins NTA-855-R1 350bhp turbocharged diesel
Auxiliary engine	1 × Cummins 6B5.9GR 75bhp with Nishinon 3-phase alternator
Transmission	1 × Niigata DW14G hydraulic torque converter, 2-speed gearbox and reverser; Goko Seisakusho final drive
Max speed	70mph
Couplers	Dellner (bar coupler within unit)
Seats	60, 71
Heating	electric
Body length	66ft 5in
Weight in wo	42.0, 41.5 tonnes
Number built	17 vehicles
Unit numbers	Not applied
Vehicle numbers	2601–17.

When first introduced, they were intended for Dublin area outer suburban services complementing the DART electric service; in line with that theme the diesel units were branded 'Arrow', a name that lasted until the 2003 livery emerged when they took on the name 'Commuter'. They added the new Dublin–Kildare suburban service to their rosters, as well as taking on longer-distance Inter-City work on the Dublin–Waterford and Limerick lines, a duty to which they were not really suited.

From early 2010, the whole class has been reallocated to Cork depot. They work commuter services from there to Cobh, Midleton and Mallow, as well as taking on stopping trains on the Mallow–Tralee line.

Above: *The two-car sets that first came to Ireland from Japan were built by Mitsui/Tokyu. Two such sets are seen passing through Dublin's Connolly station on 24 March 1995 working empty to pick up a later northbound service. These units were branded 'Arrow'.* Author

Right: *By the year 2010 most Class 2600 railcars had been concentrated on lines radiating from Cork. On 8 March 2010, cars 2614 and 2617 leave the recently-reopened station of Midleton on a commuter service for Cork.* Author

Class	IÉ 2700 railcars
Details are per vehicle:	
Designed for	Iarnród Éireann
Introduced	1998
Built by	Alsthom, Spain
Wheel arrgt	B-2
Layout	duo-directional with half-width, cab; gangwayed throughout**
Engine	1 × Cummins NTA-855-R1 350bhp turbocharged diesel
Transmission	1 × Niigata DW14G hydraulic torque converter, 2-speed gearbox and reverser
Auxiliary supply	1 × Cummins 6B5.9GR diesel / Iferca 61.5kVA alternator
Max speed	75mph
Couplers	Dellner (bar coupler within unit)
Seats	62, 50, 53*
Heating	electric
Body length	66ft 5in, 70ft 10in*
Weight in wo	38.7, 37.4, 40.2 tonnes*
Number built	25, 2 vehicles*
Unit numbers	Not applied
Vehicle numbers	2701–24, 2726, 2751,* 2753*.

*   Single railcars with two cabs.
** Unit end gangways are being removed in 2010.

Twenty-five new diesel railcars were delivered from 1998, built in Spain by Alsthom. These were a later version in the 'Arrow' theme and to a similar specification. They operate as 12 two-car units, the odd vehicle being attached to the 'spare' '2600' car to make up a further twin unit; this recently consisted of Nos 2609+2716. The '2700s' are designed to multiple with the Mitsui/Tokyu railcars though normally, apart from the hybrid set, they are run in multiple with their own kind. Two single cars were also delivered in the order. These are basically the same as the others but have a cab at each end. They can be used as strengthening vehicles with other units, or on single vehicle turns.

A feature of IÉ's second-generation diesel railcars is the use of an auxiliary diesel engine in one car that drives an alternator to provide electricity for services within the unit. In practice this equipment tends to raise the noise levels within the unit, particularly in the car under which it is mounted when the auxiliary diesel engine runs at full revolutions most of the time.

In operation the '2700' series began by working outer suburban trains north, west and south of Dublin. They also covered Inter-City workings on the Dublin–Rosslare Europort line until the Class 29000 four-car sets arrived. Later they ventured to Cork and Limerick, where they subsequently settled down to a reliable life. From 2010 they were displaced from the Cork area local trains by transferred-in '2600' sets, and the Class 2700 units have been working between Limerick and Limerick Junction, Waterford, Ennis and Ballybrophy. From April 2010 the '2700s' are the regular trains linking Limerick and Galway via the newly reopened 'western corridor' route between Ennis and Athenry at least until the '22000' railcars take over.

The Alsthom units have carried both the gold, black-and-white and the green, blue-and-white liveries. From 2010 during refurbishment the cab end gangways are being removed.

Above left: *Alsthom in Spain delivered 12 two-car units to Iarnród Éireann from 1998. Cars Nos 2703 and 2704 were undergoing commissioning at Inchicore Works on 30 October 1998. Because they came from Spain they were nicknamed 'Spanish Arrows', which was shortened to 'Sparrows'!* Author

Below: *In 2010 work began to remove the outer gangways during refurbishing at Inchicore Works. No 2718 on the left shows the new style and livery in Limerick station. On the right is 2722 with its gangway just blanked off, and No 2721 (centre) has not yet been modified.* Neil Dinnen

IÉ Class 2800 Tokyu railcars

Introduced in the year 2000, the 20 Class 2800 diesel railcars are a development of the earlier '2600' series. Like their forebears, the '2600' and '2700' series, these units are marshalled as two-car sets. They arrived in Ireland wearing the standard gold, black-and-white livery of IÉ, but were soon repainted into the green-based 'Commuter' livery. Despite that, they served for a while on long-distance services to Rosslare and Sligo, and still work commuter trains between Dublin, Mullingar and Longford. They are the preferred units on the Kildare suburban service and multiple freely with other units on the Dublin north-south corridor outer suburban services; they have moderate seating capacity and plenty of standing space for crush loading.

Like the other IÉ diesel railcars, the '2800' cars ride on non-bolster air-sprung bogies with hydraulic dampers. They have all-steel bodies and underframes, doors at 1/3rd and 2/3rd positions, and are gangwayed past each half-width driving cab. To maintain the designed braking deceleration rate, the DMUs have load-sensing equipment that adjusts the brake cylinder air pressure in proportion to the loaded weight of the car. The air pressure is maintained by a reciprocating compressor. One car in each set has a large toilet able to be used by people in wheelchairs. An additional safety feature on these units is a small pair of override buffers at the ends of the underframe. The units carry equipment for cab signalling, track-to-train control, crew radio, train communication, the so-called 'deadman's' device and driver vigilance.

The sets are normally maintained at Inchicore, but can be serviced or receive heavy repairs at the new depot at Drogheda.

Class	IÉ 2800 railcars
Details are per vehicle:	
Designed for	Iarnród Éireann
Introduced	2000
Built by	Tokyu Car Co, Japan
Wheel arrgt	B-2
Layout	duo-directional with half-width, cab; gangwayed throughout
Engine	1 × Cummins NTA-855-R1 350bhp turbocharged diesel
Auxiliary engine	1 × Cummins 6B5.9GR 75bhp with Nishinon 3-phase alternator
Transmission	1 × hydraulic
Max speed	70mph
Couplers	Dellner (bar coupler within unit)
Seats	39, 46
Heating	electric
Body length	68ft 0in
Weight in wo	43.9, 42.6 tonnes
Number built	20 vehicles
Unit numbers	Not applied
Vehicle numbers	2801–20.

The second batch of Mitsui/Tokyu railcars for Ireland began to be delivered in 2000. On 11 October 2001 a pair of these twin sets has arrived in Dublin Connolly station. These did not receive the 'Arrow' branding. All suburban DMUs were later re-liveried with the legend 'Commuter'. Author

The most successful suburban DMUs in the Irish Republic to date have been the CAF-built four-car sets of Class 29000, one of which is seen outside the new dedicated maintenance depot at Drogheda on 10 October 2005. Author

Probably the most successful commuter DMUs in the British Isles to date, the IÉ Class 29000 (delivered as Class 2900) are four-car sets, gangwayed internally but with full-width cabs in non-gangwayed fronts. The 29 sets work principally on the north-south Dublin commuter corridor as far north as Dundalk and south to Arklow and even beyond. They regularly multiple in eight-car formations, meeting the huge surge in demand for travel caused by the housing boom that arose from the 'Celtic tiger' economic boom of the late 20th/early 21st century. They also cover services on the rapidly expanding commuter routes to Longford and Maynooth, and on the line that has recently reopened part of the way towards Navan from Clonsilla. '29000s' worked Inter-City trains on the Sligo line for a couple of years before the Rotem units arrived (page 98).

The CAF units were the first DMUs to be delivered new in the lime green-based 'Commuter' livery of IÉ. They are powered by MAN 350bhp diesel engines with hydraulic transmission and have Cummins-driven auxiliary power sets. Their height, and body width of 2.9 metres, make use of the more expansive loading gauge available in Ireland on its 5ft 3in track gauge routes. While seating capacity at 185 per four-car set is moderate, standing capacity is 634 which helps with crush loadings. The author recently experienced extreme overcrowding on a Maynooth train inbound to Dublin on which he could only just squeeze and in which he felt more heavily pressed than on a Victoria Line rush hour train on the London Underground!

Class	IÉ 29000 railcars
Details are per vehicle:	
Designed for	Iarnród Éireann
Introduced	2002
Built by	CAF, Spain
Wheel arrgt	B-2
Layout	duo-directional with full-width, cab; gangwayed within unit
Engine	1 × Cummins NTA-855-R1 350bhp turbocharged diesel
Auxiliary engine	1 × Cummins 6B5.9GR 75bhp with Letga 3-phase alternator
Transmission	1 × hydraulic transmission
Max speed	75mph
Couplers	Dellner (bar coupler within unit)
Seats	40, 48, 49
Heating	electric
Body length	66ft 11in
Weight in wo	41.4 to 43.6 tonnes
Number built	116 vehicles
Unit numbers	Not applied
Original vehicle Nos	2901–80 (first 20 sets only)
Present vehicle Nos	29101–29, 29201–29, 29301–29, 29401–29.

The brand new maintenance depot in which these trains are maintained stands alongside Drogheda station. The author visited it after six months' operation to find the depot interior well equipped with state-of-the-art lifting gear for complete units. The depot was immaculately clean throughout. The depot engineer recorded that the '2900' units (as they were then classified) were delivering the highest reliability of any DMU in the British Isles.

IÉ Class 22000 Rotem railcars

Iarnród Éireann chose Rotem of South Korea to build its next batch of diesel railcars. These are three- and six-car units designed specifically for Inter-City duties. IÉ standards for Inter-City trains require a top speed of 100mph, full air-conditioning, a good and quiet ride, comfortable and spacious seating, modern décor and lighting, and accommodation for a catering trolley service and/or a buffet-restaurant car. The new Class 22000 units meet this specification well. A total of 273 vehicles was ordered and most had been delivered when this book was sent to press.

The '22000' railcars are streamlined and carry IÉ's latest green-and-grey livery for IC services. The engines are MTU, each delivering 483bhp, and they drive through Voith hydraulic transmissions. The use of separate auxiliary power units has been discarded in favour of the traction diesels driving auxiliary alternators.

Internally the trains have automatic pre-recorded announcements in the Irish and English languages and these are matched by the information screen messages at the ends of the saloons. The driver has the benefit of CCTV screens to show and record passengers alighting or boarding at platforms alongside, as well as a forward view CCTV system. The units are delivered mostly through Waterford port and then commissioned by Limerick depot. In normal service they are maintained at a specially built depot at Portlaoise, west of Dublin on the Cork main line.

Class	IÉ 22000 railcars
Details are per vehicle:	
Designed for	Iarnród Éireann
Introduced	2007
Built by	Mitsui, Japan, subcontracted to Hyundai Rotem, South Korea
Wheel arrgt	B-2
Layout	duo-directional with full-width, streamlined cab; gangwayed within unit
Engine	1 × MTU 6H 1800 R83 483bhp diesel
Transmission	1 × Voith T211re4 torque converter with dynamic retarder
Max speed	100mph
Couplers	Dellner (bar coupler within unit)
Seats	36 to 72
Heating	air-conditioned
Body length	76ft 7in (average)
Weight in wo	47.1 to 50.0 tonnes
Number built	273 vehicles
Unit numbers*	1–9, 12–63**
Vehicle Nos	22301–9/12–63; 22401–9/12–63; 22531–45; 22631–45; 22731–45; 22201–9/12–63.

* Units 1–30 and 46–63 are 3-car sets; Nos 31–40 are 6-car Inter-City-type sets and 41–45 are 6-car outer suburban units

** Three-car units 10 and 11 were returned to Rotem with severe equipment corrosion (occurred on ship). Deemed unrepairable, they are to be replaced by two additional units added to the latest order.

Operationally, the '22000s' are covering all Inter-City services other than the push-pull ones linking Dublin with Belfast and Cork. The first route to use Rotem units was Dublin–Sligo, and now the trains are seen at Rosslare, Waterford, Galway, Westport, Limerick and Tralee. The six-car units have a kitchen-restaurant car facility. The introduction of the Rotem railcars will enable IÉ to provide regular-interval two-hourly services on all these routes.

Seventeen of the three-car units are for outer suburban use around Dublin.

Top: *Two three-car sets of Class 22000, led by set 20, arrive at Dublin Connolly from Sligo on 18 May 2008.* Author

Below: *One of the six-car units, No 32, stands outside the depot at Port Laoise on 20 May 2008, during commissioning. These 100mph-sets are equipped with kitchens and buffets and can serve restaurant car meals.* Author

NIR CAF unit No 3008 approaches Belfast Central on 11 October 2005. These units caused a substantial upturn in passenger traffic on all lines on which they were introduced. Author

Delivered from 2004, the Northern Ireland Railways CAF-built three-car DMUs have made a huge impact by increasing passenger numbers immediately after being put into service. Within a year of their fleet introduction, some routes (such as Belfast–Portadown) were enjoying over 40% more custom! Such is the contrast between the public perception of the new trains and the Class 80 DEMUs (page 68) they have replaced. The Class 3000s are deployed on all NIR routes, though normally the Larne and Portrush lines are operated by older units. Six units have additional safety and signalling equipment in order to work into the Republic.

In fact the 23 'C3k' units, as they are known within NIR, are typical modern DMUs with underfloor diesel engines driving the four wheels of one bogie through a standard hydraulic transmission. With entrance doors set at 1/3rd and 2/3rd positions and with a medium-density seating layout accommodating 201 seated passengers, space for another 280 people standing, air-sprung bolsterless bogies and full air-conditioning, the Class 3000 three-car sets meet part of NIR's requirement for increased traffic volume. However, the surge in travel that resulted from their introduction meant that older DEMUs had to be kept in traffic to cope with the higher-than-envisaged passenger numbers.

With this success, NIR was able to persuade the Northern Ireland assembly to fund an additional 20 three-car units, with an option to extend them to four cars if necessary. These will be the Class 4000 DMUs. The contract was awarded again to CAF, after competitive

Class	NIR 3000	NIR 4000
Details are per vehicle:		
Designed for	Northern Ireland Railways	
Introduced	2004	2011 (planned)
Built by	CAF, Spain	CAF, Spain
Wheel arrgt	2-B	2-B
Layout	duo-directional with full-width, cab; gangwayed within unit	
Diesel engines	1 × MAN D2876 LUH03 335bhp	1 × MTU 525bhp
Transmission	hydraulic	hydraulic
Max speed	90mph	90mph
Couplers	automatic (bar coupler within unit)	automatic (bar coupler within unit)
Seats	49, 78, 58	72 (average)
Heating	air-conditioned	air-conditioned
Body length	77ft 11in, 75ft 11in	77ft average
Weight in wo	49.1, 45.0, 48.8 tonnes	46.7 t (average)
Number built/ordered	69 vehicles	60 vehicles
Unit numbers	3001–23	4001–20
Vehicle Nos	3301–23, 3401–23, 3501–23	4301-20, 4401-20, 4501-20.

tendering, and the firm is building the new units to a similar design to the '3000s' but with more powerful engines and more space inside for standees as well as more seats by dint of reducing the number of tables. Once the 'C4ks' are in service, the last DEMUs will be withdrawn, as will the last rake of locomotive-hauled stock used on suburban workings. The 'C4k' units will not multiple with the '3000' series units.

CHAPTER 13: **21ST CENTURY DEMUS**

In the livery of Virgin Trains but de-branded because Arriva was about to take over the Cross-Country franchise, a Class 220 Voyager approaches Derby on 7 November 2007 on a Dundee to Bournemouth service. Author

As part of its new Cross-Country franchise commitment, Virgin Trains initially pursued the concept of obtaining tilting DMUs for routes that needed faster curving characteristics (e.g. Banbury–Didcot and the west coast main line) and using short locomotive-worked push-pull sets on other routes. Discussions with bidding manufacturers led to a merger of the two ideas, namely a tilting DMU design and a non-tilting version of the same DMU. Bombardier was successful with its bid and moved quickly forward in arranging to assemble the four- and five-car trains in two factories, at Bruges in Belgium and in a former wagon works near Wakefield, UK.

A tilting carriage has a body that is able to rotate up to 6 or 7 degrees about a line close to its centre of gravity, the angle of tilt being determined by the amount of lateral force compensation required. These trains aim at about 60% compensation, which gives a useful speed increase of up to 20% round certain curves. The advantage is that trains can safely go round curves faster without subjecting the passengers to uncomfortable lateral forces.

The tilting version of this DMU, Class 221, needed a narrower body with sloping upper sides and a pronounced tumblehome at the bottom of the sides. This was to ensure adequate gauge clearances within the infrastructure when tilting, even if the tilt mechanism were to fail with the tilt in the wrong direction. The same body dimensions are used for the non-tilting version, Class 220, and for all subsequent developments of this type, even though a wider body design would be possible and would be more spacious internally. Having one body design for all 74 'Voyager' units was the lower cost option.

Diesel-electric 'distributed' traction was chosen for these first-ever 125mph diesel multiple-units. Each car has one 750bhp diesel engine driving a traction alternator. This feeds two underfloor traction motors. Each motor drives the nearest (inner) wheelset on each bogie through a shaft and axle gearbox. With alternating current drive, the weight of motors and unsprung mass can be kept low.

Midland Mainline (MML) opted for a version of the Class 220 for its four-car units that were to displace the original 'Turbostars' from its route. The Class 222s are known as 'Meridians'. Their superior acceleration enabled timings of the semi-fast trains to be improved. More '222s', this time of nine cars each, were ordered to enable MML's fastest services to run north of Sheffield to Leeds and to replace some HSTs. The chequered story of the 'Meridian' trains, including their subsequent changes in formations, is explained on page 102.

Hull Trains also wished to move out of 'Turbostars' on its King's Cross–Hull Paragon trains. DMUs that could do 125mph would enable service accelerations and would be easier to path on the east coast main line. They would not seat many more passengers, because a three-car '170' has almost as many seats in it as a four-car 'Voyager' type, but a faster, more comfortable and more frequent service would be possible. Thus four more four-car Class 222s were delivered. Hull Trains called these the 'Pioneers'.

All these high speed DEMUs have generally performed well. The reaction of the general public has been positive with masses more passengers being attracted to rail. Railwaymen (and retired railway engineers in particular!) tend to like them less because the travel experience is less comfortable than on the older HSTs. The noise from the '220' series engines under the floor carries inside, the carriages do not have adequate space for all needed functions, and nobody has been able to rid the 'Voyagers' of the, usually slight, whiff of toilet chemicals that greets travellers when boarding.

At the time of writing, there is talk of electrifying the Midland main line as far north as Nottingham and Sheffield. One option for trains being reviewed is to insert a transformer/pantograph car into the existing 'Meridians' so that this vehicle can feed the traction motors along the train when under the wires. Beyond the wires (e.g. en route to Burton-upon-Trent, Lincoln or York) the pantograph would be dropped, the engines started up and the train would run as a diesel-electric unit. While this would add useful capacity and would improve the travel experience by reducing engine noise over much of the route, the impact of government expenditure cuts may yet delay this idea. Nonetheless, the idea of 'hybrid' trains has caused some newspaper journalists a degree of excitement!

For a new concept, at least to the UK, the 'Voyager' series of DEMUs has been successful. True, there were some teething difficulties at the start of service, but Bombardier's support staff and that company's dedicated Central Rivers maintenance depot west of Burton-upon-Trent overcame most of them well inside the first year of operation.

The Class 220 and 221 DEMUs have scored a number of 'firsts'. They are among the first diesel multiple-units designed for 125mph. They are the first in the UK to include some units with body-tilting capability. They are equal first in using underfloor diesel engines as powerful as 750bhp. And the '220s' are the first to ride on inside-bearing, lightweight bogies and to have rheostatic braking.

The 34 Class 220 units are all in four-car formations, whereas the 44 Class 221 'Super Voyagers' are nearly all five-car sets apart from the last four. The units can multiple within and between the two classes, but not with other types of unit. The '221s' bogies are heavier wide-framed bogies, necessary to provide a platform for the tilt actuators and levers. Virgin Trains used them on services linking places as far afield as Aberdeen, Penzance and Brighton but the routes have been cut back since the franchises were relet early in the 21st century. Virgin lost the

Class	220 'Voyager'	221 'Super Voyager'
Details are per vehicle:		
Designed for	Virgin Trains franchises	
Introduced	2000	2001
Built by	Bombardier	Bombardier
Wheel arrgt	1A-A1	1A-A1
Layout	duo-directional with full-width, streamlined cab; gangwayed within unit	
Diesel engines	1 × Cummins QSK19 750bhp	1 × Cummins QSK19 750bhp
Traction motors	2 × Alstom Onix 800 3-phase motors motors	2 × Alstom Onix 800 3-phase motors
Max speed	125mph	125mph
Couplers	Dellner (bar coupler within unit)	Dellner (bar coupler within unit)
Seats	26, 60, 58, 42	26, 60, 58, 42
Heating	air-conditioned	air-conditioned
Body length	77ft 7in, 75ft 5in	77ft 7in
Weight in wo	44.5 to 48.1 tonnes	53.1, 56.6 tonnes
Number built	136 vehicles	216 vehicles
Unit numbers	220 001–34	221 101–44
Vehicle Nos	60301–34, 60701–34, 60201–34, 60401–34	60351–94, 60751–94, 60951–94, 60851–90, 60451–94

NB: All Class 220 units, and units 221 041–4 are 4-car sets. 221 101–40 are 5-car sets.

Cross-Country franchise to Arriva and the 'Voyager' fleets were split up between Cross-Country and Virgin West Coast.

Cross-Country has since determined that the use of body tilt between Banbury and Didcot does not significantly reduce journey times. On that franchisee's '221s' therefore, the tilt mechanisms have been isolated and equipment removed and stored.

Virgin, which uses the tilt capacity to maintain fast paths for '221s' between Pendolino workings on the west coast main line, continues to need the tilt system. Its units now work a new interval service from London Euston to Chester with some trains extended to Holyhead.

Above left: *A four-car 'Voyager' heads north from Stockport on the last leg of its journey from the south to Manchester. These units ride on inside-framed B.5000 bogies.* Author

Left: *A Class 221 'Super-Voyager', equipped with tilt, arrives at Derby on a Birmingham to Newcastle working on 7 November 2007. Note the outside-framed bogies which distinguish the '221' units from others of the '22X' genre.* Author

Class 222 'Meridian' and 'Pioneer'

Class	222 'Meridian' and 'Pioneer'
Details are per vehicle:	
Designed for	Midland Mainline and Hull Trains
Introduced	2003, 2005*
Built by	Bombardier
Wheel arrgt	1A-A1
Layout	duo-directional with full-width, streamlined cab; gangwayed within unit
Diesel engines	1 × Cummins QSK19 750bhp
Traction motors	2 × Alstom Onix 800 3-phase motors
Max speed	125mph
Couplers	Dellner (bar coupler within unit)
Seats	22 to 68
Heating	air-conditioned
Body length	78ft 3in, 75ft 5in
Weight in wo	46.8 to 52.8 tonnes
Number built	143 vehicles
Unit numbers	222 001–7,** 222 008–23, 221 101–4*
Vehicle Nos	60241–63, 71–4,* 60441–7, 60341–7, 60621–43, 81–4,* 60531–7, 41–7, 51–7, 71–4,* 61–7, 60161–83, 91–4,* 60918–33.

*   Hull Trains 'Pioneer' four-car units.
**   Nine-car units later reduced to eight, then seven cars.

In 2003 the first Class 222 'Meridian' four-car DEMU arrived on Midland Mainline (MML). This class was developed to replace the three-car '170s' on semi-fast workings that ran between the HST fast trains and which served intermediate stations between London, Nottingham and Derby. They were basically the same as the Class 220 design but with rearranged interiors, with the first-class area extended into an additional half vehicle. The next delivery was the first of seven nine-car units of the same class for MML's fast trains including a projected service beyond Sheffield to Leeds. This latter service did not materialise and the new units were stored for around a year.

Meanwhile in 2005 Hull Trains replaced its '170s' with a batch of four Class 222 four-car units which it marketed as 'Pioneers'. These worked services between London King's Cross and Hull. In 2009 these units were in turn displaced off the Hull route by Class 180 five-car units. The four-car 'Pioneers' went to East Midlands Trains (see below) as additional 'Meridians'.

When Midland Mainline experienced overcrowding on some of its semi-fasts, a standard-class car was removed from each nine-car set to extend seven four-car units to five cars; the longer units were entering traffic to allow transfer of some MML HSTs to other franchisees. East Midlands Trains (EMT), owned by Stagecoach, took over from MML in 2007 and in the next couple of years developed and speeded up services so that at the time of writing there are five EMT trains an hour working out of St Pancras. Three are fast to Leicester and beyond, one is semi-

fast to Nottingham, and one is a new semi-fast service to Corby. The eight-car units were soon reduced to seven cars so that the remaining nine four-car units could be made up to five cars. However, the new Corby service was only made possible by transfer to EMT of Hull Trains' four Class 222s.

Top left: *East Midlands Trains operates 16 five-car 'Meridians' on its fast and semi-fast services on the Midland main line. No 222 017 was the first to carry the new Stagecoach livery and was manoeuvring at Derby on 13 November 2007. Author*

Below left: *Soon after being reduced in length from nine to eight cars, this Up fast train was approaching Luton Airport Parkway at speed on 23 November 2006. These units were subsequently reduced to seven cars in order to strengthen the four-car units to five cars. Author*

Below: *Hull Trains 'Pioneer' unit No 222 104 leaves London King's Cross on 21 February 2007 on the 09.48 to Hull. These four units were transferred to East Midlands Trains in 2009 to initiate the London St Pancras to Corby service. Author*

In view of the development of diesel railcars that began seriously in the early 1930s, it is hardly surprising that someone would attempt to adapt existing road vehicles to run on rails as an alternative to designing something completely new. The first diesel railbus that operated reasonably long-term on railways was a Great Northern Railway (Ireland) road bus conversion. Starting life in 1934 as railcar D it had a complicated career that is described below. Other railbuses followed for the GNR(I), the Dundalk, Newry & Greenore Railway and the Sligo, Leitrim & Northern Counties Railway. The LMS (NCC) ran two road bus conversions between Coleraine and Londonderry.

These road bus conversions were aided by a piece of innovative design that emanated from the GNR(I)'s chief mechanical engineer's department, namely the Howden-Meredith wheel. Essentially, this was an arrangement whereby a rubber road tyre could be inflated inside a specially profiled steel

railway wheel tyre; a patent was lodged for the original principle and the tyre mating arrangement. Other changes necessary were to fit passenger access doorways on both sides of the vehicle as station platforms could be either side. Unlike one example on the LMS railway in the UK, these railbuses were not road-railers in that, once they had been converted for railway operation, they could not be used on the roads. They were intended to be a cheap solution to the ongoing problem of lowering costs on railways with little traffic. The author is not aware of any of these vehicles being supplied new, all being converted from buses that had seen service on the roads of Ireland, though at least one received a newer body later in its life. All of these vehicles had one driving cab and so needed to be turned at the end of each journey. Many survived in service into the 1960s. The driving cabs of most of the railbuses were

half-width to give better access to the engine compartment.

At a time when roads were generally rough-surfaced and sometimes potholed, it was possible to achieve a slightly more comfortable ride by using these vehicles on the railway. The insertion of a rubber tyre between the outer tyre and the vehicle suspension, however, resulted in these vehicles not working track circuits reliably and so disappearing from signalbox panels. The GNR(I) solved this by modifying some railbuses with steel front wheels. This would have done nothing to improve the ride! On most Irish branch lines, track circuits were non-existent and the use of Howden-Meredith wheels continued.

Leyland Motors in 1934 built three four-wheeled double-ended railbuses for the LMS, which lasted until 1951. Later, as part of its 1955 modernisation plan, BR issued a similar specification to several firms to supply small numbers of railbuses that would have driving cabs at both ends and be suitable for low-traffic branch lines. One design came from Germany, but not from the company that manufactured Deutsche Bundesbahn's well-known Uerdingen railbuses. The four other types were from British factories. Their introduction did little to attract many passengers. The ride was hard, accommodation limited, and all had been withdrawn by the end of 1968. Three other vehicles were acquired by BR for departmental use, one from Wickham being a clone of the passenger ones, and two from Drewry being overhead line inspection vehicles.

Vehicle ride was always going to be a problem when attempting to design small railcars to run on just two axles, at least until suspension design had been developed through the British Railways Research department from which sprung the 'Pacer' suspension system. These prototypes, introduced between 1978 and 1984, are described in Appendix 1.

Above: *The Howden-Meredith wheel was not just a rubber tyre within a properly-profiled steel one. This view shows the protection afforded by guide bars at the front and back of the wheel, which were intended to avoid derailment in the unlikely event of a puncture. The assembly enabled a more or less acceptable ride on the railway to be obtained from a converted road bus. GNR(I)/IRRS*

Left: *The pioneer diesel railbus identified as 'D' shows how basically simple the conversion was. Apart from the Howden-Meredith wheels, the body has an additional passenger doorway in the opposite side from the original to allow access from platforms on either side. There are also low-level steps. L. Hyland/IRRS*

GNR(I), NCC and CIÉ bus conversions

Ireland eventually hosted 12 railbuses that had been converted from older road buses, though some were replacements for railbuses damaged at level crossings or in collisions so not all were extant at the same time.

GNR(I) railbuses D and E emerged from Dundalk Works in 1934 having been converted from road buses run by the railway. They were renumbered D1 and E2 in 1936 to make way for new diesel railcars D and E. In 1939 railbus D1 was sold to the SL&NCR to replace the latter's damaged railbus A (see next page). Railbus E2 was renumbered 1 in 1939; in 1956, it became CIÉ service inspection railbus No 8178. It lasted long enough to be preserved as GNR(I) No 1 and is at Cultra.

In 1935 railbus F emerged, becoming F3 in 1938, but was destroyed in an accident in 1944. A replacement was provided the same year, only to be renumbered 2 in 1947; in 1958 CIÉ took it over and scrapped it in 1960. Also in 1935, the GNR(I) provided two railbus conversions for the Dundalk, Newry & Greenore Railway, that line's Nos 1 and 2.

Diesel railbuses				
Designed for	**GNR(I)**	**DN&GR**	**LMS (NCC)**	**CIÉ**
Introduced	1934	1935	1934	1953
Converted by	Dundalk	Dundalk	NCC	CIÉ
Wheel arrgt	1A	1A	1A	1A
Max speed	c30mph	c30mph	c30mph	c30mph
Seats	28, 31	28, 30	c30	c30
Weight in wo	6 tons	c6 tons	c6 tons	c6 tons
Number built	5*	2	2	1
Vehicle Nos.	D/D1 (later SL&NCR A), E/E2/1/8178, F/F3, F3/2	1, 2 (later GNR(I) 3, 4**)	42, 41 or 43	2508
Layout	uni-directional with half-width cab			
Diesel engine	1 × Gardner 4LW 62bhp			
Transmission	manual gearbox and clutch			
Coupler	rear hook to tow luggage trolley			
Heating	engine waste heat.			

* Includes replacement for original F3 damaged in accident.
** GNR(I) railbus 4 became CIÉ service railbus 8177.

These became GNR(I) Nos 3 and 4 in 1948. No 3 was withdrawn in 1955 and the other became CIÉ service railbus No 8177. All the GNR(I) railbuses carried the handsome royal blue-and-cream livery also used on the company's road buses and diesel railcars.

Most of these railbuses used Gardner 4LW diesel engines of 62 to 68bhp. Whether or not the LMS (NCC) railbuses converted in 1934 and 1936 with Howden-Meredith wheels were diesel or petrol driven is not clear. Also, CIÉ's conversion in 1953 of a 1934-built AEC Regal IV road bus to produce railbus No 2508 was probably also a petrol-engined vehicle. It saw two years' use on the Thurles–Clonmel line before being stored and then withdrawn in 1961.

Above: *GNR(I) railbus No 2 had its leading pneumatic-tyred wheels replaced by simple steel ones, as seen at Dundalk depot in July 1957. This was done to improve the operation of low-voltage electric track circuits.* Author

Right: *LMS (NCC) railbus No 42 was one of two on that railway that continued the use of Howden-Meredith wheels.* IRRS

While not originating the principle or carrying out the conversions, the 5ft 3in-gauge Sligo, Leitrim & Northern Counties Railway made good use of railbuses from 1935 until the line closed in 1957. Every day one railbus would make the early morning 48-mile journey from Enniskillen to Sligo, and pick up the return working in the middle of the day. The railway was impecunious and laid on light track, so the use of four-wheeled railbuses provided a service while having little impact on the track. Two railbuses were in stock during the period from 1938 to the closure of the railway.

The first railbus was a conversion made to order by the GNR(I) at its Dundalk Works. SL&NCR railbus A was a four-wheeled, full-width-cab, petrol-driven vehicle seating 32 passengers. Unusually it had the passenger entrances at the rear on both sides. To achieve greater fuel economy, the engine was changed to a diesel in 1938, the vehicle receiving a Gardner 4LW. To carry luggage, the SL&NCR provided the railbus with a small covered four-wheeled trailer, looking somewhat like a 'henhouse on wheels'! Unfortunately railbus A was damaged beyond economic repair in an accident in 1939. Quick action was taken that year to replace railbus A by obtaining from the GNR(I) the latter's railbus D1 and repainting it in SL&NCR green-and-white livery, taking the same designation, railbus A, the body retaining its access doors at the front of the saloon sides. This vehicle survived until the railway closed, though it was little used in its last years.

The SL&NCR purchased a new railbus conversion from Dundalk Works in 1938 and this was designated railbus 2A. This was rebodied in 1950 with a more modern body with half-width cab. The passenger entrance doors were at the rear on this railbus. No 2A continued to be the basic service provider right through to the end of the railway in September 1957. Both railbuses were scrapped after the railway closed.

SL&NCR diesel railbuses

Converted for	SL&NCR	GNR(I)	SL&NCR
Vehicle No	A	A	2A
Introduced	1934	1939*	1938
Wheel arrgt	1A	1A	1A
Max speed	c30mph	c30mph	c30mph
Seats	32	29	32
Weight in wo	c6 tons	6 tons	c6 tons
Layout	uni-directional with full-width cab**		
Diesel engine	1 × Gardner 4LW 68bhp		
Transmission	manual gearbox and clutch		
Coupler	rear hook to tow luggage trolley		
Heating	engine waste heat.		

NB: All vehicles converted by GNR(I) at Dundalk Works. No 2A was rebodied in 1950.

*   Second-hand vehicle, formerly GNR(I) No D1 converted in 1934.

**   Original railbus A. The second railbus A and No 2A had half-width driving cabs.

Left: The SL&NCR painted its railbuses two-tone green with white roofs. This is the replacement railbus A with a full passenger payload. IRRS

Below: When the second railbus A was rebodied, in its new form it had the passenger entrances on a platform at the back of the vehicle. This is how it looked in May 1957. The railbuses normally towed small wagons for luggage and parcels traffic. J. G. Dewing/Colour-Rail

Bottom: Railbus 2A was similar to the rebodied railbus A. It stands ready to leave Enniskillen station. There is some GNRB mahogany stock in the background. IRRS

LMS Leyland railbuses

At the beginning of 1934, Leyland Motors delivered to the LMS three four-wheeled railcars that pre-dated the BR 1958-built railbuses by 24 years yet were clearly the inspiration for them. Here was a two-cab, 40-seat, 13-ton railbus with a maximum speed of 56mph driven by a 110bhp underfloor diesel engine, almost exactly the pattern that BR followed with its modernisation plan railbuses nearly a quarter of a century later.

The vehicles used Leyland's long experience of building bus bodies. Internally there were 40 seats, in 2 + 2 rows, facing the nearest driving cab through which passengers had an excellent view forwards or backwards. There was a sliding access door halfway along each bodyside. Livery was maroon with cream bands. The body was set on an all-welded steel underframe with a wheelbase of 21ft. This was supported on four 11-leaf springs above the axleboxes which were held in place by longitudinal rods; small horn guides steadied the car during acceleration and braking. Braking was by compressed air. Small buffers and drawhooks at each end were purely to enable the railbuses to be towed for whatever reason. The LMS set stringent operating rules for these cars, including the need, when being towed, for someone on board to operate the handbrake whenever required. Other operating rules recognised that these railbuses were unable reliably to work track circuits.

The railbuses began their service life in summer 1934 working out of Blackburn towards both Spring Vale and Clitheroe, two cars being allocated to Lower Darwen shed for this purpose. The third car went to Scotland where, based at Hamilton depot, it worked on several of the lightly-trafficked branch lines in the Ayrshire coal mining area. In

Class	Leyland diesel railbuses
Designed for	LMS
Introduced	1934*
Built by	Leyland Motors Ltd
Wheel arrgt	1A
Layout	duo-directional with two half-width cabs
Engine	1 × Leyland 6-cylinder 95bhp diesel
Transmission	1 × Lysholm-Smith torque converter; reversing final drive
Max speed	56mph
Coupling code	no multiple facility
Seats	49
Heating	not known
Underframe	41ft 1in
Weight in wo	13 tons 2cwt
Number built	3
LMS numbers	29950–2

* Built in 1933.

the 1940s the other two cars joined the one at Hamilton. Two were out of traffic by 1949, being a source of spares for the one working the Hamilton–Holytown service. All were withdrawn by BR in 1951.

Below: *While it is not certain whether UR7924 had a petrol or diesel engine in it, the LMS road-railbus is worth illustrating just in case! This followed a different concept from the Irish railbuses in that the bus had separate road and rail wheels side by side. When on the road, the rail wheels would be raised clear of the road surface and the bus was driven normally. This was a trial vehicle, seen here on what appears to be an official trip.* National Railway Museum

Above left: *Of a completely different concept, No 29950 was one of the four-wheeled Leyland railbuses used on the LMS between 1933 and 1949. These were similar in basic layout to the railbuses purchased by BR in the 1950s. They served in Lancashire and in Scotland.* Ian Allan library

Of the 22 four-wheeled diesel railbuses ordered by British Railways in its modernisation plan, five each came from four manufacturers, and two from another. Strictly they were four-wheeled diesel railcars, not being road bus conversions and not having any obvious road vehicle design characteristics. The idea of buying so few railbuses from so many sources was a feature of BR's modernisation plan, aimed at concentrating future orders on the best vehicles. In the case of the railbuses, future orders did not transpire.

The vehicles delivered by AC Cars Ltd had wide access doors centrally located on the bodysides, with additional steps for access to very low platforms. The lightweight mild steel body was supported on the underframe by four rubber-bonded corner springs. The underframe was in turn supported by rubber-bonded sandwich springs, two at each axlebox arranged at opposing angles so that spring compression increased rapidly in proportion to vertical track forces. Thus there was little 'give' in the primary suspension, leaving the vehicles with a tendency to dip into rail joints and to hunt on straight track.

The 150bhp BUT diesel engine drove one axle through the standard railcar arrangement of fluid coupling and four-speed gearbox. Brakes were straight air, supplied by Clayton Dewandre. To save weight, the vehicles did not have traditional side buffers and couplings but had small hooks for emergency towing and light metal sprung defenders where contact might occur when colliding with other vehicles' buffers. At 11 tons, the AC Cars railbuses achieved the lightest weight of any in the series.

They were employed on minor branch lines in Scotland and on the Western Region. The last car was withdrawn in 1968. Three survived into preservation, though one was broken up rather than face the cost

Class	AC Cars diesel railbuses
Designed for	BR
Introduced	1958
Built by	AC Cars Ltd
Wheel arrgt	1A
Layout	duo-directional with two half-width cabs
Engine	1 × AEC 6-cylinder 150bhp diesel
Transmission	1 × Wilson 4-speed gearbox; reversing final drive
Max speed	55mph
Coupling code	no multiple facility
Seats	46
Heating	Smith's oil-fired warm air heater
Underframe	36ft
Weight in wo	11 tons 0cwt
Number built	5
BR numbers	79975–9.

of asbestos insulation removal. The sole survivor is on the Colne Valley Railway.

AC Cars railbus No W79976 was stabled at Swindon on New Year's Day 1961. Note the low-level steps below the passenger entrance; these could be extended outwards for use at ground-level halts. The railbus has buffered up to the steam locomotive on the left, showing its sprung defenders in contact with the buffers of a steam locomotive. Author

Not the most reliable railbuses on BR, the Bristol pair worked fitfully in Scotland for eight years. No SC79958 undergoes attention at Aviemore in September 1958. D.A. Kelso/Colour-Rail

Possibly the smartest-looking BR railbuses were the two that emerged from the Bristol/Eastern Coachworks consortium in 1958. The two companies had been part of the Tilling Group that the British Transport Commission had taken over on nationalisation. The Bristol railbuses followed the standard BR specification for vehicles designed to work low-income branch lines economically. The idea of small railbuses had already taken root in Germany and neighbouring countries, and BR officers thought that their low-cost of operation, perhaps even single-manning, would save the lives of threatened branches.

These vehicles had integral bodies clad in aluminium to save weight. The wheels were of the resilient type from Svenska Aktiebolaget Bromsregulator in Sweden. Each axlebox supported a sub-frame through rubber springs. The sub-frame in turn supported the main underframe, also through Metalastic springs, paralleled by hydraulic dampers to cut down any tendency to bounce. The engine was a Gardner 6HLW 112bhp diesel and it drove one axle through a fluid coupling and a fully-automatic SCG five-speed gearbox.

Braking was innovative as it used an unusual form of air/hydraulic-operated disc braking with a separate cylinder and clasp unit for each wheel. There was also a scrubber block at the top of each wheel to clean the tread and to aid detection by track circuits.

Class	Bristol/ECW diesel railbuses
Designed for	BR
Introduced	1958
Built by	Bristol Commercial Vehicles and Eastern Coach Works Ltd
Wheel arrgt	1A
Layout	duo-directional with two half-width cabs
Engine	1 × Gardner 6HLW 6-cylinder 112bhp diesel
Transmission	1 × SCG 5-speed automatic gearbox; reversing final drive
Max speed	55mph
Coupling code	no multiple facility
Seats	56
Heating	Smith's oil-fired warm air heater
Underframe	42ft 4in
Weight in wo	13 tons 10cwt
Number built	2
BR numbers	79958–9.

The two vehicles were painted BR dark green and had bright metal lines and end flashes rather than the standard cream painted lines and warning 'whiskers'. The cabs were half-width and partially open to the passenger saloon.

The two Bristol railbuses worked in Scotland, firstly on the Speyside line and the Beith branch. Both cars ended up at Hamilton and worked in Ayrshire, and both showed signs of increasing unreliability, not uncommon among such small classes of individual vehicles. They were both withdrawn in October 1966, having been replaced by standard DMUs.

These five all-steel railbuses had an unusual design of body suspension. The bottom corners of the vehicle body were outside and slightly below the outer corners of the underframe. The body hung from the underframe corners by four coil springs, each of which was paralleled by a Woodhead Monroe hydraulic damper to prevent resonant oscillation. Primary suspension was by long, thin leaf springs below the axleboxes and suspended by hangers from the underframe. There were no horn guides, the axleboxes being held in place by the springs themselves.

The direct-acting air brake was of the Clayton Dewandre pneumatic type with clasp brake blocks on the wheels. Wheelsets were standard BR 3ft-diameter wheels. The engine was the normal horizontal AEC diesel of 150bhp output and it drove a typical sequence of cardan shafts through a fluid coupling and an SCG four-speed gearbox.

The Park Royal cars incorporated a two-digit headcode panel at each body end, as well as two marker lamps and a destination blind. Livery was BR dark green with cream lining and warning 'whiskers'.

Three Park Royal railbuses were used on the London Midland Region in the Bedford area, and the other two in Scotland. The latter's duties included Ayr–Kilmarnock services, the Dalmellington branch and the Speyside line; they also ventured on to the Craigendoran–Arrochar shuttle service. The two Scottish vehicles had drop-down steps for passenger access to ground-level platforms. By 1960 all was not well with some of these cars, two of them having serious frame fractures. Withdrawals began late in 1966, with the last going early in 1968. None is preserved.

Class	Park Royal diesel railbuses
Designed for	BR
Introduced	1958
Built by	Park Royal Vehicles
Wheel arrgt	1A
Layout	duo-directional with two half-width cabs
Engine	1 × AEC 6-cylinder 150bhp diesel
Transmission	1 × SCG 4-speed epicyclic gearbox; reversing final drive
Max speed	55mph
Coupling code	no multiple facility
Seats	50
Heating	Smith's oil-fired warm air heater
Underframe	42ft 0in
Weight in wo	15 tons 0cwt
Number built	5
BR numbers	79970–4.

It is a matter for conjecture whether a railway with passenger traffic that is so sparse as can be accommodated in a small vehicle with only 50 seats can ever be viable. Suffice it to say that most services worked by BR's diesel railbuses of all types were withdrawn during the 1960s, making the railbuses themselves redundant even though they were all relatively new.

Park Royal railbus No SC79970 is at Craigellachie in July 1960, ready to depart for Aviemore. C.J. Gammell/Colour-Rail

BR Wickham railbuses

The small Hertfordshire company of Wickham had a contract to supply five railbuses to the BR specification. Its factory was limited in space, but all five were produced during 1958. Interesting features of this design included the method of suspension. The primary suspension used semi-elliptic springs under the axleboxes. Each axlebox was located at the end of a horizontal steel arm bracketed from the underframe with rubber bushes at the ends. Each axlebox was damped by a Woodhead Monroe damper. The body was located on the steel underframe with six Cushyfoot rubber mountings. These were resilient; they cushioned vertical bumps and resisted lateral displacement. The overall effect was a better vehicle ride than was achieved on the other railbus designs.

The cars each had a Meadows 105bhp diesel engine driving one axle through a multi-disc mechanical clutch and a Wilson four-speed gearbox. The off-centre side doors could be accessed from low platforms using retractable steps.

No 79968 experimentally had an automatic gear change system which the driver could switch out if needing to go back to manually-initiated gear changes. No 79969 had André Westinghouse pneumatic suspension instead of conventional axlebox springing.

In service, in common with some of the other designs of BR railbus, they suffered from frame fractures. This was possibly exacerbated by the secondary line track they were expected to negotiate. The five Wickham cars were used in Scotland, including work on the Alloa–Kinross line,

Class	Wickham diesel railbuses
Designed for	BR
Introduced	1958
Built by	D Wickham & Co Ltd
Wheel arrgt	1A
Layout	duo-directional with two half-width cabs
Engine	1 × Meadows 6-cylinder 105bhp diesel
Transmission	1 × disc clutch and Wilson 4-speed epicyclic gearbox; reversing final drive
Max speed	55mph
Coupling code	no multiple facility
Seats	44
Heating	Smith's oil-fired warm air heater
Underframe	38ft 0in
Weight in wo	11 tons 5cwt, 24 tons*
Number built	6
BR numbers	79965–9, DB999507*.

* Departmental track-recording vehicle, introduced 1959. Speed limited to 30mph when recording.

the Speyside line out of Aviemore, and between Craigendoran Upper and Arrochar. Withdrawals began as early as 1963, with the last being condemned in 1966. The auto-gear-change car, 79968, was withdrawn after fire damage.

A sixth Wickham railbus was built in 1959 for departmental service. It carried probes for more accurate track alignment recording than could be achieved by manual observation and the on-board equipment enabled comparisons to be made directly with runs carried out earlier. The car rejoiced under the name Elliott, the name of the company that led the overall design concept of the track recording equipment. This vehicle is the only Wickham railbus to be preserved. It is now on the Lavender Line at Isfield.

Left: *In its early years as a track recording car, the Wickham railbus DB999507 was rather garishly painted in canary yellow (lower panels) and buff above. It carried its track recording equipment on a prominent frame below solebar level. 'The Wickham' later assumed the name Elliott and gained blue-and-red colours. In preservation it is in lined BR dark green.* P.J. Sharpe

Right: *The Wickham railbuses were smart-looking vehicles. No SC79965 awaits departure from Crieff for Gleneagles in July 1961.* George M. Staddon/Colour-Rail

It is not now clear why BR contracted the German firm of Waggon und Maschinenbau, GmbH to build five railbuses, rather than Uerdingen who had about 700 examples already in service on the continent. However, the resultant design from WMD was well arranged albeit with differences from the British-built examples. The most obvious change was the inclusion of a full set of side buffers, drawgear and hose connections rather than the light buffing springs and end hooks of the others. Thus it was possible for these cars to work coupled together in tandem, though this only appears to have been done regularly since they were preserved.

These cars had more conventional axlebox guides, but lined with frictionless composite material to enable the axleboxes to move freely. They were supported by laminated springs suspended from the underframe. The body was supported elastically at four points on the underframe. The ride on these cars was reported as being good.

Heating was partly by engine coolant running through pipes in the saloon, but there was also a Webasto air heater. These cars were unique among BR's DMU mechanicals in not having free-wheels.

Their field of operation was almost entirely in East Anglia where, at that time, there was a number of under-used secondary and branch lines. Reliability was variable. The author has read of occasions when passengers needed to help push-start a railbus when the battery had run down. The Buessing diesel engines also had reliability problems. On cars Nos 79961/3/4 these engines were replaced by standard AEC engines. Withdrawal was completed by the end of 1967.

Class	WMD diesel railbuses
Designed for	BR
Introduced	1958
Built by	Waggon und Maschinenbau, GmbH
Wheel arrgt	1A
Layout	duo-directional with two half-width cabs
Engine	1 × Buessing 6-cylinder 150bhp diesel
Transmission	1 × disc clutch and ZF electro-magnetic 6-speed gearbox; reversing final drive
Max speed	55mph
Coupling code	no multiple facility
Seats	56
Heating	waste engine coolant heat; Wabasto oil-fired warm air heater
Underframe	41ft 10in
Weight in wo	15 tons 0cwt
Number built	5
BR numbers	79960–4.

Four out of the five survive in preservation. Nos 79962 and 79964 are on the Keighley & Worth Valley Railway in Yorkshire, where they have run many times their BR mileage in service! Nos 79960 and 79963 are on the North Norfolk Railway.

Above: *The German examples came from WMD – not, surprisingly, from Uerdingen. This is No E79964 at Newcastle on 13 August 1965.* Peter Swift

Left: *Two of the four preserved WMD railbuses have covered very many more miles in the service of the Keighley & Worth Valley Railway than they ever did for British Railways! This one is at Keighley on 7 January 1989.* Peter Swift

Ryde Pier trams

It was unusual, but not unique, for British Railways to inherit a tramway. It did, after all, own the Grimsby to Immingham tramway. But BR's ownership of the Ryde Pier tramway is perhaps less well known. Ryde was the main port of embarkation for travellers to and from the Isle of Wight, being conveniently opposite Portsmouth and Southsea. Because of the shallow waters, Ryde Pier is very long at 2,250feet.

It is in fact three piers side by side. The first pier was the promenade pier which had a wood plank walkway to enable travellers to reach the ferries. This was opened in 1814, and subsequently extended at various times to reach its present length. The tramway pier, parallel and just to the east of the promenade pier, was opened in 1864 and the trams were horse-drawn until electrification came in 1885, one of the earliest in the world and using a conductor rail. The tramway for many decades ran south of the pier into the town of Ryde, but was cut back to Esplanade at around the time the adjacent railway pier opened, it being decided that the railway, with Ryde's third station at St John's Road, served the back of the town effectively enough.

The pier tramway had two parallel tracks. Early photographs show crossover connections between them but in later decades one tram and trailer ran independently on each track. In high season both trams would shuttle between the buffer stops at Ryde Esplanade and the Pier Head terminus. At times of low traffic only one tram was used.

The electric trams were replaced by petrol-driven Drewry four-wheeled trams in 1927. These were converted to diesel in 1959. BR repainted them from Southern Railway malachite green to carmine red after nationalisation; they reverted to BR Southern carriage green later on. The tramcars and the trailers had two axles and a driving position at the outer end. The tramway closed in 1969 and the trams were then dismantled.

The two Ryde Pier tramway power cars were refitted in 1959 with diesel engines, thus requiring them to be recorded in this compendium!
This view shows No 1 hauling its trailer en route from the Pier Head to Esplanade station on 30 August 1953, six years before the conversion which did not change the vehicles' appearance. Author

Described in this appendix are vehicles that probed the design possibilities for diesel railcars and units but which were built in limited numbers or had short lives.

LMS diesel electric train

The London Midland & Scottish Railway pursued the idea of using diesels for rail traction in several ways. One was expressed in the conversion in 1927–28 of four coaches from a former Lancashire & Yorkshire Railway electric multiple-unit that had been withdrawn from service when the Holcombe Brook branch was de-electrified. One vehicle was rebuilt as a diesel-electric power car. Inside a compartment near the cab end of the vehicle was a Beardmore 500bhp diesel engine coupled to an English Electric 600Volts dc generator which had a separate exciter. The engine was a slow-speed heavy design with cylinders of 8¼inch diameter and 12inch stroke. The engine and generator were bolted to a common bed-plate. The exciter also supplied auxiliaries including battery charging. There were two traction motors, fitted to the rear end bogie of the power car to help spread the weight more evenly. The motor bogie was from a Euston–Watford electric multiple-unit.

Trials were run on the Blackpool–Lytham section during 1928 and 1929. Problems arose with the diesel engine, its governor, and even a crankshaft breakage. The crankshaft was alleged to have been under strain because of the way the bed-plate was bolted directly to the underframe, the modern system of three-point mounting having not been established at that time. A report showed that the costs of running this train had been higher than an equivalent steam push-pull train. The LMS concluded, in conjunction with the power train suppliers, that the diesel engine could not easily be modified to give the reliability required and that the high cost of keeping it running could not be justified.

Class	LMS diesel-electric train
Designed for	LMS
Introduced	1928
Rebuilt by	LMS, Horwich Works & Newton Heath
Wheel arrgt	2-B (power car)
Layout	4-car bogie unit with one power car at one end and driving trailer at the other
Engine	1 × Beardmore 8-cylinder 500bhp diesel
Transmission	English Electric 600V dc generator; 2 × 280hp traction motors
Max speed	not known
Coupling code	no multiple facility
Seats	297 (4-car train)
Heating	electric
Weight in wo	144 tons (59+26.5+26.5+32)
Number rebuilt	1
LMS numbers	14570, 14668, 14669, 14571.

The train was withdrawn in 1931, about the time that Beardmore's diesel engine factory closed for good. The train pre-dated Ireland's first diesel railcar by three years. It was the first diesel-electric unit train in the UK, and would not be followed by another using the same concept (if one ignores single railcars) until the 'Hastings' units began to emerge in 1957 (page 64).

A project undertaken in 1927 by the Dick Kerr works of English Electric launched the UK's first ever diesel-powered unit passenger train using former Lancashire & Yorkshire Railway EMU stock. GEC

Armstrong Whitworth and English Electric railcars

From 1931 Armstrong Whitworth built three new diesel railcars for evaluation. These were 60ft-long bogie cars with a cab at each end and were designed to haul a single trailer vehicle if needed. They were diesel-electric vehicles, each with a Sulzer engine of 250bhp coupled to a Lawrence Scott dc generator feeding two GEC traction motors. With a maximum speed of 65mph and capacity to carry 60 passengers in a high-density seating arrangement, they were potentially useful vehicles. The carriage bodies were supplied by Cravens Ltd of Sheffield, and were of all-steel construction. The power unit was floor-mounted behind one driving cab. The radiator was on the roof above the engine room.

The first car was named Tyneside Venturer and painted blue-and-cream. The second and third vehicles were Lady Hamilton and Northumbrian. All three were built as demonstrators, the first two aimed at the LNER and the third at the Southern Railway which did try it for a season. In fact all three were purchased by the LNER during 1932 and 1933. For a few months in 1933 Northumbrian worked on the LMS carrying the name Armstrong Shell Express; fitted out as a luxury vehicle with 12 plush seats, it carried VIPs between London Euston and the British Industries Fair at Castle Bromwich. It reverted to standard seating before being sold. During scheduled overhauls the LNER repainted the mailcars green-and-white. They worked around the North-East, based at Heaton depot in Newcastle.

Armstrong Whitworth built a fourth railcar to a much lighter-weight specification. This was an underfloor-engined diesel-electric which appeared in 1933, and this, too, was bought by the LNER which used it as a back-up for the other three. Unreliability was its problem, and it was withdrawn in 1938. The whole group of four had been withdrawn by the end of 1939, and scrapped by 1944.

In parallel, English Electric pooled the resources of three of its factories to build in 1933 a diesel-electric railcar to a similar layout to the first Armstrong cars. This vehicle was called Bluebird and went on trial on the LMS. It had an above-floor 200bhp high-speed engine and a top speed of 60mph, which it achieved during trial running early in 1934, but no purchaser came forward.

AW and EE diesel electric railbuses			
	Named railcars	**Unnamed railcar**	**EE railcar**
Designed for	Demonstrator	Demonstrator	Demonstrator
Introduced	1931	1933	1933
Assembled	Armstrong Whitworth*	Armstrong W*	EE Dick Kerr works
Wheel arrgt	B-2	B-2	B-2
Max speed	60mph	60mph	60mph
Seats	60**	57	53
Weight in wo	42 tons 10cwt	17 tons 10cwt	37 tons 10cwt
Layout	duo-directional with 2 × cabs	duo-directional with 2 × cabs	duo-directional with 2 × cabs
Diesel engine	1 × Sulzer 250bhp	1 × Saurer 95bhp	1 × EE6H 200bhp
Transmission	GEC dc electric	dc electric	EE dc electric
Traction motors	2 × GEC	1 × ***	2 × EE 100hp
Underframe	60ft	52ft 6in	61ft 6in
Buffers/coupling	Std side/centre	Lightweight	Std side/centre
Heating	electric	electric	electric
LNER numbers	25, 232, 224	294	—
Vehicle names	Tyneside Venturer, Lady Hamilton, Northumbrian**	None	Bluebird

*   Bodies supplied by Cravens Ltd, Sheffield (named cars), Park Royal (294).
** Northumbrian worked on the LMS for 3 months as Armstrong Shell Express with 12 luxury seats. Reverted to normal in 1934.
*** No 294 had 1 underfloor traction motor with shaft drive to 2 axles on 1 bogie.

Right: *The Armstrong Whitworth diesel electric railcar No 232, Northumbrian, was to the same basic design as the next two that were delivered, all ending up on the LNER around Newcastle upon Tyne.* National Railway Museum

Below: *The fourth Armstrong Whitworth railcar, LNER No 294, was a lightweight vehicle which was not designed to haul extra carriages.* Ian Allan library

Below right: *The English Electric Bluebird was a diesel-electric railcar similar to the Armstrong Whitworth cars in layout. Its coil-spring secondary suspension looks advanced for 1933.* English Electric Co

The Ganz railcar became UTA No 5 in 1951 and was photographed at Belfast York Road depot in July 1957. Author

Metropolitan-Vickers built a double-ended diesel railcar in 1937 which did some evaluation running on the LMS main line out of Euston, but which was then put aside for many years. The railcar was based on a Ganz (Hungary) design that had been used successfully between Budapest and Wien (Vienna) and was generally known as the 'Arpád' type. With a maximum speed of 70mph, the MetroVick vehicle had a vertical diesel engine of Ganz design, made in the UK under licence. The engine was mounted on one bogie, in a space behind the nearest driving cab, but encroaching on an otherwise usable area within the body. After the trials, the LMS took no further interest in it and it was stored.

After its formation in 1949 the Ulster Transport Authority in Northern Ireland was considering the use of diesel railcars and purchased the MetroVick/Ganz vehicle for its own use in 1951. The vehicle was regauged to 5ft 3in and given the fleet number 5. In operation No 5 worked on both the former Belfast & County Down lines and on the Northern Counties Committee routes. Apparently its performance did not compare well with the four ex-NCC railcars (see page 25).

However, the railcar remained in occasional service, ending up on the Portrush branch line where it settled down to some useful work. UTA had provided an air-braked trailer coach to work with it, a converted ex-LMS (NCC) vehicle, though this probably reduced performance to a minimal level. The trailer car, No 215, later renumbered 515, had no driving cab and thus railcar 5 needed to run round it at the end of each

UTA Ganz railcar	
Designed for	Demonstrator
Introduced	1937*
Built by	Metropolitan-Vickers**
Wheel arrgt	B-2
Max speed	70mph
Seats	54
Weight in wo	38 tons
Layout	duo-directional with 2 × full-width cabs
Diesel engine	1 × Ganz 215bhp***
Transmission	mechanical
Underframe	64ft
UTA number	5.

*   Acquired by UTA and regauged in 1951
**   Probably assembled by Metropolitan-Cammell at Washwood Heath, Birmingham
*** One source gives engine power of 250bhp, but actual performance suggests the 215bhp figure (based on the Hungarian and Romanian railcars of this type) is more likely to be correct.

journey. No 5 was transferred to the GNR section from around 1958 but was stored there until scrapped in 1965. Its trailer vehicle was inserted into a MED set (see page 28).

An 'Arpád' railcar is preserved in Hungary, and about 17 similar vehicles are still in use in Romania.

LMS articulated diesel unit

Intended to probe the prospects for using a fleet of diesel trains on a variety of duties and meet certain key criteria, the LMS built a streamlined, articulated three-car unit in 1938. To maximise route availability it had to be of light weight. But the minimum axle-load was set at 10 tons to ensure the train worked track circuits successfully. Thus it was essential to use articulation to keep down the number of axles. The form of articulation was original. The three carriages rested on four bogies. The two inner bogies had conventional centres; each of these centres carried the middle of a 15ft-long longitudinal beam. The outer ends of this beam carried the pivots on which the ends of the adjacent carriage bodies rested. The geometry of this arrangement enabled the lengths of the carriages to be longer than more conventional articulation methods, such as on the LNER. The weight of the carriage ends was carried directly on the bogies through rollers. A development of this layout was used in the first prototype Advanced Passenger Train four decades later.

The carriage bodies were timber-framed and bolted to the steel underframes, and were skinned with welded steel plate. The underframe design used a deep central truss, either side of which were cantilevered the diesel engine brackets. Each engine (there were two under each car) drove through a torque converter, switching to direct drive above a set speed. Engine speeds, reversing shifts and other controls were executed through electro-pneumatic valves, not unlike on the first-generation BR DMUs. The unit had a straight air brake. Carriage heating was by condensing steam radiators warmed in boilers by the engine exhaust gases.

Passenger sliding doors had push-button operation, effective only when the guard had released them. Interlocking prevented the train being driven with a door open.

After trials the unit worked between Oxford and Cambridge. From 1939 it worked services between St Pancras and Nottingham. Based at Bedford,

it was stored during the war. The two end cars were later converted to form part of an overhead wiring train. These were observed derelict at Longsight in 1967.

LMS articulated diesel unit	
NB: Details for complete unit:	
Designed for	LMS
Built by	LMS Derby
Introduced	1938
Wheel arrgt	1A-Bo-Bo-A1
Max speed	75mph
Seats	162
Weight in wo	73 tons
Layout	duo-directional with 2 × full-width streamlined cabs; 3 cars articulated
Diesel engines	6 × Leyland 125bhp
Transmissions	Leyland Lysholm Smith torque converter and direct drive
Heating	Engine exhaust heat condensing boilers feeding steam to radiators in saloons
Unit length	164ft 6in
Buffers/couplings	Lightweight, for rescue only
Vehicle Nos.	80000–2.

The LMS streamlined articulated railcar set was painted in a striking livery of bright red and cream. In this posed view it carries oil headlamps denoting an express train. R. G. Jarvis

Class	ACV diesel units
Designed for	Demonstration
Introduced	1953
Built by	ACV Ltd
Wheel arrgt	1A
Layout	duo-directional with two half-width cabs
Engine	1 × AEC 6-cylinder 125bhp diesel
Transmission	1 × fluid coupling and 4-speed epicyclic gearbox; reversing final drive
Max speed	50mph
Coupling code	no code; multiple within ACV type only
Seats	28 to 52
Heating	oil-fired warm air heater
Underframe	37ft 6in
Weight in wo	13 tons 0cwt
Number built	11
BR numbers	79740–50.

Until BR had fully established its programme for bogie DMUs the railways of Britain were regarded as fertile ground for promotion of different manufacturers' prototypes. The well-known company AEC had changed its commercial name to ACV Ltd (Associated Commercial Vehicles) in 1948 though its diesel engine and road vehicle products were still badged 'AEC'.

In 1953 ACV launched an experimental three-car lightweight diesel train of two-axle vehicles for trials on BR as a possible solution to the pressing problem of enabling otherwise uneconomic passenger services to survive. The unit consisted of two power cars and one intermediate trailer. Each power car had two cabs and one AEC 125bhp underfloor diesel engine driving through a four-speed epicyclic gearbox and a reversing double-reduction final drive on one axle. The layout was such that the train could be used as a three-car unit, a power-twin or as two single vehicles.

BR purchased the train in 1955 and later that year bought a second batch consisting of five power cars and three trailers, effectively a four-car and three-car set with a spare power car. These were painted in BR lined green. The second batch differed in detail from the first: the later

units had no lower side fairings, and had sliding windows instead of droplights.

The ACV cars were tested on all BR regions but mainly worked Watford–St Albans and Harrow–Belmont services. Unpopular through a hard ride (nicknamed 'the Flying Bricks'!), and prone to increasing failures, the units were sidelined and eventually all stored near Derby Friargate. A few had been transferred to the civil engineer's department in 1959 but apparently had been little used. All were broken up at Derby by the end of 1963.

Above left: *Near Amlwch on Anglesey in 1953 is a train of first-batch ACV cars in grey livery and with bottom skirts.* W. G. Rear/Colour-Rail

Below: *A set of three ACV four-wheeled railcars from the second batch arrives at Watford on 10 September 1958. This set has no side skirt panels and is painted in standard BR dark green.* P. J. Sharpe

BR/Paxman diesel-electric unit

The BR/LMR/Paxman diesel-electric experimental units No 9821 and 9828 were photographed leaving Carlisle on a test run on 10 July 1957.
J. N. Faulkner

Class	BR/Paxman diesel-electric unit
Details are for two-car unit:	
Designed for	testing
Introduced	1956
Rebuilt by	BR Derby
Layout	2-car duo-directional unit with full-width cab at each end
Engine	2 × Paxman ZH 6-cylinder 450bhp diesels
Transmission	2 × BTH dc generators; 4 × traction motors
Max speed	85mph
Underframe	57ft each vehicle
Coupling code	no multiple facility
Weight in wo	103 tons
Number rebuilt	2 vehicles
BR numbers	9821, 9828.

In 1954 Paxman Diesels Ltd developed a horizontal engine for potential use as an underfloor railcar engine. This was coded ZH and was effectively one cylinder bank from the company's established 12-cylinder YH Vee-engine. To test its suitability for a railcar application BR provided two old LMS carriages and fitted a ZH engine under each of them. Electric traction equipment was purchased from British Thomson-Houston. Motor bogies came from former LMS Euston–Watford electric multiple-units. At 450bhp, the engine was expected to provide a lively on-track performance.

Each carriage was fitted out with a driving cab at one end with three front windscreens and a marker lamp at the top. The train was painted in BR's standard dark green lined livery, even with front 'speed whiskers'.

The two-car unit began trials in 1956 and these carried on for about 17 months. To the author's ear, the trials were largely successful, the train being tested up to its design maximum speed of 85mph.

For the record, a variant of this ZH engine was used six years later in the BR Clayton Type 1 diesel-electric locomotives which had one engine at either end.

UTA railcars 6 and 7

The UTA prototype railcars Nos 6 and 7 were successful vehicles and proved that the authority could rebuild existing carriages into diesel railcars. These had horizontal engines and mechanical transmissions, and were photographed at Belfast Queen's Quay terminus. Desmond Coakham/IRRS

Class	UTA Nos 6 and 7
Designed for	Development
Introduced	1951
Built by	UTA Duncrue Street
Wheel arrgt	1A-A1
Layout	duo-directional with one full-width cab
Engine	2 × AEC 6-cylinder 125bhp diesel
Transmission	2 × fluid coupling and 4-speed epicyclic gearbox; reversing final drive
Coupling code	no multiple facility
Seats	73, 120 (trailer)
Heating	oil-fired steam boiler
Underframe	60ft 0in
Weight in wo	35 tons 0cwt
Number built	2 (+ 1 trailer)
UTA numbers	6, 7, 279/528 (trailer).

Looking forward to an early time when it would need a fleet of modern DMUs for suburban working, the Ulster Transport Authority converted two pre-war NCC passenger carriages into diesel railcars. These were numbered 6 and 7 and entered service in 1951.

Converted at Belfast Duncrue Street works, near York Road locomotive works, Nos 6 and 7 were unusual in being the first classic diesel railcars in Ireland to use horizontal underfloor diesel engines. The engines were 125bhp AEC engines and they each drove through a fluid coupling and a four-speed epicyclic gearbox, the final drive being positioned in the middle of the nearest axle and not at the end of the axle as was the case with the GWR, GNR(I) and the CIÉ railcars. In this respect Nos 6 and 7 set the tone for British Railways' mechanical DMU fleet. The cars had the

Gresham & Craven quick-release vacuum brake. No 6 contained an oil-fired boiler which fed steam to all the heaters in the unit.

The railcars retained the slam doors of the original carriages. The new seating was in a 2+3 suburban layout giving 73 seats per car. UTA also provided an intermediate trailer car, converted from 1933-built slam-door suburban coach No 279, later renumbered 528, which added 120 more seats. The intermediate coach was non-gangwayed.

The unit performed well, sometimes as a two-car and sometimes as a three-car train. It mainly worked on the Bangor line until the advent of the MED units (page 28) for which it provided useful experience. Later it worked out of Belfast Great Victoria Street on services to Lisburn, then out of York Road on the Larne line. The two railcars were withdrawn in 1966, and destroyed in a fire in 1969. Trailer 528 carried on in service, probably in MED units, until its withdrawal in 1971.

In the early 1970s, as the first-generation DMUs aged, it became clear to BR that an up-to-date replacement design or designs would be necessary. BR was not in a flush financial situation and indeed neither was the country as a whole. Any DMU replacements had to be cheap.

BR Research had been studying the wheel-rail interface from fundamental principles. Its experimental high speed freight wagon chassis had been successfully towed at 100mph with no resonant hunting. An idea came forward that a simple standard road bus body could be mounted on a similar chassis and a diesel traction system fitted to the underframe producing a low-cost four-wheeled railbus. Thus was born LEV1, the initials 'LEV' standing for 'light experimental vehicle'.

The bus body chosen was the Leyland National which was regarded at the time as the model example for cheap, mass construction of road vehicles. The body was flexibly mounted on the chassis, fitted with two cabs with no end gangways and had one wide passenger access doorway on each side. Its road bus genesis meant that the body was narrower than conventional rail vehicles. LEV1 was thoroughly tested while not actually entering commercial passenger service.

The key to the acceptable vehicle ride was the suspension. Each axlebox casing incorporated seatings for long, flexible, vertical coil

springs. The tops of these springs supported the vehicle underframe directly. Lateral movement of the axleboxes was restrained by lateral dampers and vertical bounce was held in check by one vertical damper outside each axlebox. The axlebox was held firmly in longitudinal position by a rod parallel to the track that linked, through rubber-bonded bushes, the axlebox plank with a bracket off the underframe. Thus the axlebox could move up and down to follow rail alignment and side to side to cope with lateral impacts but not fore and aft; thus axle hunting was avoided.

Other development prototypes soon followed, on longer chassis. One of these, LEV2, was successful enough to be sold to a USA railroad and is now exhibited in Connecticut, and one ended up in service on Northern Ireland Railways, mainly on the Portrush branch. That vehicle (formerly RB3) is now on display in the Ulster Folk and Transport Museum at Cultra near Belfast. The fourth railbus (RB4), built in 1984 at Workington, was fitted with air-conditioning during a short spell in the USA and now operates on the Telford Steam Railway.

The natural development of these vehicles was the 'Pacer' series of DMUs, starting with the Class 140 prototype (next page).

Above right: The original prototype railbus from BR Research, No LEV1 was based at the Railway Technical Centre, Derby, where it was photographed on 3 November 1982. Author

Above: The third prototype railbus was this one, which was later sold to Northern Ireland Railways who used it on the Portrush branch shuttle to and from Coleraine. BRB

Right: RB4 had a similar layout except that it had centre and end doors. It was on the Mickleover test rack at Derby in May 1984. Peter Swift

BR Class 140 DMU

In 1981 the railbus-based two-car DMU emerged as an operational prototype in BR stock. No 140 001 was tested on several BR regions including a prolonged spell on scheduled trains in the Strathclyde PTE area around Glasgow and also in West Yorkshire. It was a two-car unit, again with Leyland bus body-sections making up its narrow body. The two bodies were gangwayed between them, and there was provision for staff to pass between adjacent units if in multiple though this was never used. The Leyland engine and transmission presaged the future for BR DMUs. The engine drove through an automatic gearbox, taking the unit up to a maximum speed of 75mph. The suspension was a development of that under the prototype railbuses (page 119). Unlike first-generation DMUs, the '140' was air-braked.

Inside the unit had a linoleum floor and bus-type seats. A toilet was fitted at one end of one car. Each car had two passenger entrance doorways on one side and one on the other, giving three entrances on each side of the two-car unit. Heating was by waste heat from the engines being used to heat fresh air that was fan-driven into the saloons. The vehicle ends had mechanical automatic couplers. The body ends were utilitarian in the extreme, being flat-fronted with a recessed gangway door and with the multiple connections hung from below the front windscreens, a visually untidy arrangement. A pair of two-tone horns was prominently placed on the cab roof. The livery was royal blue below the waist and off white above.

During its running in Scotland, which the author experienced several times, the unit ran smoothly on continuously-welded main line track but dipped and swayed when negotiating jointed track on secondary lines, a ride feature now well known through wide experience of the later Classes 141 to 144 (pages 74-8).

After withdrawal in 1981 and a period of storage, 140 001 was purchased privately and sometimes operates on the Keith & Dufftown Railway.

Class	140 DMU
Details are per vehicle:	
Designed for	BR
Introduced	1980
Built by	BREL/Leyland Motors
Wheel arrgt	1-A
Layout	duo-directional with full-width cab; gangwayed within unit
Engines	1 × Leyland TL11 205bhp diesel
Transmissions	1 × Self-Change Gears mechanical gearbox; Gmeinder final drive
Max speed	75mph
Couplers	automatic (bar coupler within unit)
Seats	50
Heating	waste heat from engine system
Body length	52ft 6in
Weight in wo	19 tons
Number built	2 vehicles
Unit number	140 001
Vehicle numbers	55500–1.

Above right: The suspension of the Class 140 unit used a long horizontal link with flexible rubber end bushes to hold the bottom of the axlebox in alignment with the track and two flexible coil springs in parallel with a vertical damper. Author

Right: The prototype 'Pacer' unit No 140 001 stands at Springburn station on a working for Cumbernauld in 1981. The unit was tried on several BR regions. Author

It is often stated that the Class 210 diesel-electric prototype units were 'engineering led' whereas a more sensible solution to DMU replacement would have resulted if the project had been 'marketing led' from the outset. The author can testify that the project was indeed led by BR's passenger marketing department, at least initially. That department called the initial meeting that gathered together all the relevant departments and regional representatives. That the diesel-electric option was chosen came from this meeting and was no doubt a knee-jerk reaction to the early recognition that the 'Pacer' concept with two axles and underfloor engines was unsuitable for longer journeys.

On offer was a multiple-unit train based on the Class 317 EMU that BR had successfully built for the Bedford–London services. It was not difficult for the engineers to put a high-speed lightweight diesel generator set in a power car, using the same bogies and electric traction equipment as in the EMU, and this idea was accepted for development of two prototype trains. Performance had to match that of an EMU, and the potential for a DEMU and EMU to work in multiple was to be explored.

The power units chosen for comparison were the Paxman 6RP200L (in effect half an HST engine) and the MTU 12V 396 TC. Each was located within the vehicle body behind the driving cab of an end car. Corridor access was possible past the engine room, unlike the Southern Region DEMUs before them. The layout of the coaches was similar to EMUs with double sliding doors in the bodysides at 1/3rd and 2/3rd positions. 210 001 had outer-suburban seating, and 210 002 inner-suburban high-density. 210 001 was a four-car set and the other a three-car unit, the Paxman engine being in the three-car unit. They were both gangwayed throughout.

The '210' DEMUs had a 90mph top speed and performed well in service. They spent time on several BR regions, including covering

Class	210 DEMUs
Designed for	Evaluation
Introduced	1981
Built by	BREL Derby
Wheel arrgt	B-B (power cars)
Layout	4-car and 3-car duo-directional units with half-width cabs at each end and gangwayed throughout
Engine	1 × Paxman 6RP200L 6-cylinder 1,125bhp diesel 1 × MTU 12V 396 TC 12-cylinder 1,140bhp diesel
Transmission	1 × dc generator; 4 × traction motors
Max speed	90mph
Veh length	65ft
Couplings	BSI (bar couplings within units)
Seats	254, 203
Heating	electric
Weight in wo	64.5, 25.5, 29.5 tons
Number built	1 × 4-car, 1 × 3-car
Unit numbers	210 001–2
Vehicle numbers	60200–1, 60300–1, 60400–1, 60450.

medium-distance services in Scotland, before being allocated to Paddington suburban workings on the Western Region. They were withdrawn in 1985 after the future was seen to be with the 'Sprinter' type of DMU (page 80). Some of the carriages were later used in Class 455-type EMUs.

The four-car version of the Class 210, No 001, leaves London Paddington and passes Royal Oak LU station on a Down suburban working in July 1983. Author

Metro-Cammell Class 151 DMU

A Metro-Cammell 'Sprinter' prototype unit, No 151 001, has just arrived at Derby from Matlock on 18 September 1985. Author

Metro-Cammell paralleled BREL in introducing two prototype three-car DMUs in 1985. The Metro-Cammell offering was a lighter-weight unit with bodies made of welded aluminium extrusions. These were left unpainted, apart from lining, decals and cab fronts. Bogies were Metro-Cammell's own design. The power train was the same Cummins diesel engine but driving through a Twin-Disc torque converter incorporating a direct drive above about 40mph. A cardan shaft took the drive to a Gmeinder final drive on the inner bogie, and a short shaft brought the drive to the other pair of wheels on the same bogie. Unusually for the UK, the cooling radiators were on the roof of each vehicle.

The units were tried in traffic and based at Derby for a season, mainly on the Matlock line. Difficulty in arranging smooth gear changes was part of their ultimate downfall. The BREL '150' was proving to be smoother riding, with better gear changes; it was more reliable, and was soon chosen for quantity production. The '151s' were withdrawn in 1989 by BR's Regional Railways business sector as non-standard and stored at Llandudno Junction.

Serco decided to buy them for possible use as test vehicles; it stored them near Derby until a company called Endeavour Rail purchased them. They were then moved to the LNWR depot at Crewe, but the idea that they would be used for spot hire to train operators who were short of stock did not come to fruition. The units were cut up at Crewe in 2004.

Class	Metro-Cammell Class 151 DMUs
Designed for	Evaluation
Introduced	1985
Built by	Metro-Cammell, Washwood Heath
Wheel arrgt	2-B
Layout	3-car duo-directional units with full-width cabs at each end and gangwayed within units
Engine	1 × Cummins NT855 285bhp diesel
Transmission	1 × Twin-Disc 1330 torque converter; Gmeinder final drive
Max speed	75mph
Veh length	65ft 6in
Couplings	BSI (bar couplings within units)
Seats	68, 84, 80
Heating	waste heat from engine system; oil-fired supplementary heater
Weight in wo	32 tons 6cwt (average)
Number built	2 × 3-car
Unit numbers	151 001–2*
Vehicle numbers	55202–3, 55302–3, 55402–3.

* Renumbered 151 003–4 in 1987 to avoid overlap with 150 001–2.

Iris 1 and Iris 2

The Railway Technical Centre at Derby was home to several BR engineering departments including BR Research as well as mechanical and civil engineering. In the reorganisations of the 1980s that preceded privatisation, BR set up Central Services to, among other things, manage the non-commercial rolling stock fleet. Under privatisation in 1997 Serco, the well-known service provider group, bought out parts of Central Services and set up its own test section called Serco Railtest.

When by 1969 the single Derby 'lightweight' railcar No 79900 had been withdrawn from revenue traffic, it was converted for BR Research as a laboratory car and known as Iris, later becoming Iris 1 when Iris 2 took to the rails. Iris 1 was used as a radio survey vehicle and for work such as gauging the infrastructure. Inside there was a diesel generator set for

Above right: The transfer of single Derby 'lightweight' railcar No 79900 into departmental stock secured its future for eventual preservation. It is seen at Basingstoke as RDB975010, labelled Test Coach Iris. David Cable

Below: Iris 2 was converted from a Class 101 Met-Cam unit and was also used for infrastructure surveys and gauging work. Unit 901 002 was at Derby on 4 March 2004 after upgrade work and repainting into Network Rail's yellow livery. Author

Bottom: When Iris 1 was preserved, the Midland Railway Centre at Butterley rebuilt it close to its original form as M79900. It now works on the Ecclesbourne Valley Railway, Wirksworth. Author

supplying auxiliary power mainly for instrumentation, and there was also a kitchen and seating for staff. It was painted in the Research Division's livery of red-and-blue carrying the number RDB977010, though much later was repainted in its original BR dark green with yellow warning panel.

When Iris 1 was retired it was restored faithfully to near original condition at the Midland Railway Centre, Butterley, and now works passenger trains on the Ecclesbourne Valley Railway near Derby.

Iris 2 was a Class 101 twin unit (vehicles 53222 and 53338) that was converted in 1991 for similar duties. It became unit 950 002 with car numbers 977692+977693. One car carried a diesel alternator set and had an air-conditioned section to house sensitive instrumentation. Originally painted in Railtrack's green-and-blue colours, the unit ended its departmental life in Network Rail's all-over yellow. Retired in 2007, under preservation it has moved to the West Somerset Railway.

Other DMU departmental conversions

Left: *The laboratory car RDB975385 was called Hydra because it was used to test hydrostatic transmission. It was photographed on BR Research Department's Mickleover test track in the early 1980s.* Colin Marsden

Below left: *Hydra was an adaptation of Cravens-built Class 129 parcels car No 55997 and was painted in the red and rail-blue livery of BR Research.* Peter Swift

Below: *Railtrack, in the Chiltern Railways area, used former Class 121 single railcar No 55024 as a track-treatment vehicle for applying Sandite paste to the rail heads to improve adhesion in the leaf-fall season. It was unusually painted in former BR maroon, as seen at Aylesbury depot on 10 April 2000.* Author

At least 30 DMU sets from the first-generation BR fleet have at different times been converted for use in departmental stock. Some eight of these are still in service at the time of writing, in most cases appearing to undertake seasonal work such as applying Sandite paste to rails to improve adhesion during the autumn 'leaf fall' season.

One unique vehicle was the Cravens single parcels car No 55997 which was converted in 1980 to test hydrostatic drive. Becoming RDB975385, the vehicle was named Laboratory 9 Hydra. One of its Leyland engines was coupled to two Rexroth Hydromatic axial piston pumps. Each pump supplied hydrostatic oil at 400bar (about 6,000lbf/sq in) to a motor that drove one axle directly. The vehicle was a test bed for the drive and was, to the author's knowledge, only the second rail vehicle to have such a drive in this country (see Locomotive Compendium: Southern, page 119, for the other). After a few years' testing, Hydra was scrapped.

The withdrawal of the single-car Classes 121 and 122 vehicles led to a rash of them being brought into departmental stock for duties such as route learning and track treatment. No 55029 was converted in 2001 as a video survey vehicle and is used to help Network Rail catalogue its infrastructure. It is still in service as 977968, painted in NR's standard yellow livery.

Fifteen Classes 121/122 single cars have been in departmental stock. Eight of these were equipped for Sandite duties, of which four are still doing that. Two (977975/6, formerly 55027/31) spent some years as Severn Tunnel emergency vehicles, but are now in store. The rest have been used for route learning. Most have been preserved and are popular on heritage railways as being relatively cheap to run at periods of low traffic.

Odd units are a '117' that serves as a water-cannon unit to clear the rail heads of the mulched remains of fallen leaves. This was formed from power cars 51371, 51375 and 51413, becoming 977987, 977992 and 977988 respectively. Three '107' power-twins were converted in 1991 as Sandite units in Scotland. 977830–5 were renumbered from 51990, 51993, 52005, 52012, 52025 and 52030 though not in that order. These went into preservation at the end of their tour of duty from 1996.

Class 114 twin Nos 55929 (parcels car numbering) and 54904 was used as an automatic train protection test train from 1991 numbered 97775/6. It was withdrawn in 2002 and is now preserved. A Class 103 Park Royal unit, 50397+56160, was in departmental stock from 1971 to 1985 as 975137 and 975228.

Five Class 101 Metro-Cammell units also served as Sandite units and have since either been scrapped or preserved. Like the others now withdrawn, their duties were taken over by new multi-purpose units built by Windhoff.

Lastly one must mention five ex-Southern Region DEMUs that spent time in departmental stock in the 1990s, mainly as Sandite units. Only one survives at the time of writing, unit 930 301 formed out of 60145, 60660 and 60149.

Iris 1 (page 123) was not the only Derby 'lightweight' DMU to have an extended life in departmental service. Converted in 1968 was a two-car unit made up from vehicles 79018 and 79612. This was equipped as an ultrasonic rail test train, and was able to check rails for cracks whilst on the move. It remained on this duty through to 1995, when it was withdrawn carrying the numbers RDB975007 and RDB975008. The unit is now preserved and is being restored at Butterley.

The replacement for the former ultrasonic test train was Class 101 unit 51433+53267. This was significantly rebuilt in 1986 for its new purpose, and included former 4REP driving motor car 62483 as an intermediate trailer. The unit had air brakes throughout. It was registered as unit No 901 001 with vehicles 977391+999602+997392. The unit has recently been withdrawn and the power cars are now on the Churnet Valley Railway.

Unit 950 001 was built by BREL at Derby Litchurch Lane works in 1987 using the basic form of a Class 150 two-car unit but modified for its specific purpose as a track assessment train. The two cars are numbered 999600 and 999601. The unit carries laser and video equipment to measure and record the track on which it runs. Regular runs over the network enable technicians and engineers to compare records over the years to determine the rate of deterioration of track, and thus to be able to prepare programmes for future track repairs and renewals. Being more or less a standard DMU, the unit has a wide route availability. Whereas the high-speed measurement train based on an HST set is used to record the state of Britain's main lines, this DMU can cover the secondary routes, necessarily at wider intervals that acknowledge the slower rate of change of track alignment on these routes.

Unit 950 001 is based at the Railway Technical Centre (now known as the rtc Business Park) at Derby and is owned and operated by Network Rail.

Left: *The Derby 'lightweight' two-car unit RDB975007-8, used as an ultrasonic rail test train, is seen in October 1975 at Oldbury in the West Midlands.* David Cable/Colour-Rail

Below: *Network Rail's track measurement train based on the Class 150 type two-car DMU is unit No 950 001 and has vehicles Nos 999600 and 999601. It was at Derby station when caught by the camera on 27 June 2002.* Author

Drewry inspection vehicles

Class	Drewry inspection vehicle
Designed for	LNER
Introduced	1950
Built by	Drewry Car Co*
Wheel arrgt	1 A
Layout	duo-directional vehicle with full-width cabs at one end and half-width section at the other, plus staff reach tower
Engine	1 × diesel
Transmission	mechanical
Max speed	23mph
Vehicle length	29ft
Couplings	side buffers and central drawhook
Equipment	reach tower for OHL inspection
Weight in wo	16 tons 10cwt
Number built	2
Works numbers	2267–8
BR numbers	original not known/DB998900–1.

* One report states constructed by Baguley of Burton-upon-Trent.

The LNER ordered two overhead line inspection railbuses from the Drewry Car Co in 1947. Held up by the nationalisation of railways, the cars were not delivered until 1950. One was originally intended to support the Woodhead route electrification; the other was for the Great Eastern. They had Drewry works numbers 2267 and 2268.

Each vehicle was a four-wheeler with a half-width section at one end allowing space for a lifting platform in which staff could be raised to reach the overhead wiring. The vehicles could be driven from either end. The diesel engine drive is geared for a maximum speed of 23mph, sufficient for inspection work but rather slow when needing to clear the main line! The cars were delivered in a grey livery.

In 1977 the two railcars were taken into stock by BR's Research Department as they were needed to help maintain the overhead line on the division's test track at Old Dalby. They were numbered DB998900/1. By this time No 998900 was in poor condition, but was able to provide spares to make 998901 operational. No 998901 was painted in the Research Department's red-and-blue colours. Ten years later it was repainted into the newer grey-and-red colours.

Ten years after that, in 1997, the two vehicles were available for sale by Serco Railtest which had no further use for them. The EM2 Locomotive Society purchased them with a view to making one operational vehicle from the two. This was done, and 998901 is at the Middleton Railway, Leeds, resplendent in BR lined dark green where it sees occasional use at periods of low traffic volume.

Above: Hard at work adjusting the overhead electric line on the Old Dalby test track is the Drewry diesel vehicle 998901. The raised access platform sits on the vehicle underframe alongside the half-width driving cab at the opposite end of the car. David Coxon

Below: No 998901 was preserved and restored by the EM2 Locomotive Society in view of its early history relating to the MSW line. The vehicle is now on the Middleton Railway and is painted lined BR dark green. Ian Dobson

APPENDIX 3: **PEOPLE MOVERS**

Class 139 Parry people mover

After decades of demonstrating prototypes and upgrading them in the light of experience, the Parry people mover concept was adopted by the London Midland franchise in 2009 by the acquisition of two vehicles for the Stourbridge Junction to Stourbridge Town short branch line. Not strictly diesel railbuses since they use liquid petroleum gas as their primary fuel source, the two Parry people-movers are aimed at a low-cost solution to low-volume traffic flows. The engine in each four-wheeled car is a 2.3litre Ford DSG423. The drive is hybrid and uses braking energy to accelerate a high-speed flywheel that can rotate up to 2,600rpm. Energy from the flywheel drives the car, supplemented by output from the Ford engine which is much smaller than would be needed if it was the sole traction engine. Each car weighs 12tonnes and has a maximum speed of 40mph.

Class	139 Parry people mover
Designed for	London Midland
Built/introduced	2008/2009
Built by	Parry People Movers Ltd*
Wheel arrgt.	1 A
Layout	duo-directional vehicle with two driving positions in passenger saloon
Engine	1 x Ford DSG423 2.3litres LPG engine
Flywheel	diameter 1metre; mass 500kg; operating range 1,000 to 2,600rpm
Transmission	4 V-belt drive to flywheel; Linde two-way hydrostatic transmission and gearbox drive from flywheel to axle
Braking	mechanical drive to flywheel; emergency disc brake
Max. speed	40mph
Vehicle length	31ft
Seats	25
Couplings	central towing bracket and pin
Weight in w.o.	12tons
Number built	2
Vehicle numbers	39001-2
Unit numbers	139 001-2

* Underframes supplied by Alan Keef Ltd

No 139 001 was working the service on 5th February 2009 when photographed at Stourbridge Town. The vehicle manages a return trip on the branch line every ten minutes! Author

Bibliography

Books and magazines

The author consulted many sources to gather the information in this Compendium. The most useful are listed here and are recommended for further reading.

ABC British Railways Locomotives & Locoshed Book 1959, summer 1959 edition, published by Ian Allan Ltd. A lot of basic DMU detail and dimensions listed here.

British Railways Locomotives & Coaching Stock 1993, published 1993 by Platform 5 Publishing Ltd, ISBN 1 872524 49 4. Basic DMU detail and dimensions tabulated.

The British Railcar by R. M. Tufnell, published in 1984 by David & Charles (Publishers) Ltd, ISBN 0 7153 8529 1. Very useful background on older railcars.

British Railcars 1900–1950 by David Jenkinson and Barry C. Lane, published 1996 by Atlantic Transport Publishers, ISBN 0 906899 64 8. A wide-ranging survey of steam, petrol and diesel railcars during the first half-century of their existence.

Diesel Dawn by Colm Flanagan, published 2003 by Colourpoint Books, ISBN 1 904242 08 1. Explains Ireland's important contributions to the development of diesel railcars and DMUs in the British Isles.

LMS Diesel Locomotives and Railcars by E. V. Richards, published 1996 by the Railway Correspondence and Travel Society, ISBN 0 901115 76 2. Thoroughly researched coverage of all diesel-driven rail vehicles introduced by the LMS.

The Locomotive, 15 June 1928, article headed Diesel-Electric Train, L.M.& S. Ry. Probably the definitive surviving description of the pioneering conversion of an ex-L&YR EMU into the UK's first diesel unit train.

Websites

The author also found several websites useful and lists some here for readers to dip into.

Research Division index. Lists most departmental diesel units operated from Derby's Railway Technical Centre from BR's time. Find it at: www.traintesting.com/R&DD_index.htm

The Railcar Association. This website is becoming the definitive internet source of information and data about DMUs in the UK. Go to: www.railcar.co.uk/index.htm

The Railway Centre.com has a useful listing of BR and later DMUs by class and gives copious data on them. www.therailwaycentre.com/New%20TRC%20Main%20Pages/DMU_index.html

Wikipedia. What would we do without Wikipedia? While acknowledging that its pages have some irritating gaps in information, it is nonetheless a useful source and has some valuable information on DMUs, even though the data needs to be cross-referenced where possible. Go to: http://en.Wikipedia.org/wiki/List_of_British_Rail_diesel_multiple_unit_classes

Index

Right: *On 25 March 1977, a Western Region Class 117 DMU passes Ufton Nervet on an outer-suburban working, probably to Newbury.* Alan Thorpe

Below: *Class 170s had a relatively short stint working for South West Trains. Including No 170 308 – seen reversing at Romsey on the shuttle service to Totton on 2 December 2005 – all were transferred to ScotRail; SWT now uses refurbished Class 158s on services such as this.* Author